Reading for Ideas

Reading
for
IDEAS

Walter Pauk
Director of Reading-Study Center
Cornell University

Josephine M. Wilson
Head of Department of English
Odessa-Montour Central School

David McKay Company, Inc.
New York

Reading for Ideas

ISBN: 0-679-30244-1

Library of Congress Catalog Card Number 73-92520

Manufactured in the United States of America

To Laurie, who is always more fascinated by ideas than by facts

Preface

There are few things more discouraging than putting forth a great deal of hard work, but coming up with very little to show for it. In reading literature, as well as in other endeavors, anything can be done better by system than by haphazard. The system will be explained in the following section.

We want to express our appreciation to the many people whose encouragement and material aid have made this book possible. Appreciation is also expressed to the authors and publishers for their permission to reprint the selections of which they hold copyright. Our students, in the classroom and in seminars, have taught us much, and we are grateful to all of them.

Special acknowledgment is due the late Mr. Edward Wilson for his editorial advice and wise counsel.

Finally, we are grateful to Mrs. Laura Relyea for her competent and always willing assistance in carrying the major burden in the preparation of the manuscript.

Walter Pauk

Ithaca, New York

Josephine M. Wilson

Clearwater, Florida

To the Student

If anyone is in a position to give advice on how to read literature, it is Dr. Mortimer J. Adler who is the main force behind the Great Books movement. After years of teaching and writing about reading, Dr. Adler's advice to those who want to improve boils down to this: *keep awake!* But, let him tell his own story. In *The Challenge of the Twentieth Century*, he states:

> All the skill or know-how needed for reading a worth-while book, and especially a great book, can be boiled down to *knowing how to keep awake while reading.* This involves more than keeping one's eyes open and remaining more or less conscious with a book in one's hand. It means keeping one's mind open and actively at work in the process of learning. The more active one is in reading, the more one stands to learn, for the more one puts one's mind into the book, the more one's mind takes from it.

One sure-fire way to put Dr. Adler's advice to work for you, is to ask questions while you read—questions that you yourself try to answer in the course of reading. The better the book, the more it will help you by provoking questions in your mind and challenging you to find and weigh the answers.

Questioning not only keeps your mind awake, but also keeps it from becoming flabby. The following story makes this point in a memorable way.

To keep their fish alive for the fresh-fish markets, the owners of fishing trawlers invented a water-filled, floating tank. The fish remained alive all right, but they were never firm, always flabby and stale. One captain, however, always brought back firm, fresh, lively fish. His fish always commanded a higher price. One day he revealed his secret: "You see," he said, "for every hundred herrings I put into my tank, I put in one catfish. It is true that the catfish eat five or six of the herrings on the trip back to port, but the catfish keep the rest alert and constantly moving. That's why my herring arrive in beautiful condition."

The reading system in this book is based on question-asking. Hopefully, the questions will do the work of the catfish: keep you alert, lively, and in good mental condition.

Contents

Reading for Ideas

Reading for Ideas

Introduction

In this program, twenty selections, excerpted from outstanding literary works, provide realistic practice material. Following each selection are six types of questions revolving around the basic elements essential for comprehending literature. In addition, there is an Instructor's Guide that analyzes the questions and discusses the answers to them.

THE SELECTIONS

The selections that comprise this book were chosen from novels or short stories. These selections are not haphazard "snippets"; rather, each episode tells a story in its own right. Care was taken to choose material from outstanding books that are usually assigned for reading in literature courses.

SIX TYPES OF QUESTIONS

The set of questions at the end of each selection is designed to teach the following comprehension skills: (1) Understanding the Author's Use of Words, (2) Understanding the Author's Use of Figurative Language, (3) Recognizing Traits of Character, (4) Recognizing Tone, (5) Recognizing the Author's Theme or Themes, and (6) Recognizing Development of the Theme.

These six types of questions are asked concerning each selection. By striking repeatedly at these essential concepts, we hope to create a pattern of questioning that may henceforth become a habitual way of reading literature.

1. Understanding the Author's Use of Words

A noted linguist, S. I. Hayakawa, once said that "no word ever has exactly the same meaning twice." He was basing this statement on the idea that the precise meaning of a word depends on the context in which it is used. Furthermore, he maintains that no two contexts are ever exactly the same; so, we should always study the meaning of a particular word in its specific context.

The mistake that many students make is to look up an unfamiliar word in the dictionary, then take the first or most popular definition they run across. As we know, most words have several definitions; some have several dozens. To select the definition that most precisely fits the word, a good policy to follow is this: Take the number-one definition given by the dictionary; then, read the sentence in which the unfamiliar word is used, but substitute the dictionary definition for the word itself. Judge for yourself whether or not the substitution makes sense. If the sentence does not make sense, try another definition. Do this until you believe that you have finally found the right substitution.

An example of a word that has many definitions is "take." Surely, we do not mean the same thing when we say, "I plan to *take* my books to school," as when we say, "I plan to *take* the bus to school." In the first case, we mean *carry*, and in the second case we mean *ride*.

2. Understanding the Author's Use of Figurative Language

When asked to interpret the figurative language of an author, students often hesitate, erroneously thinking that their own interpretations are too obvious.

Most students become quite expert in their interpretations after they learn that the purpose of figurative language is to make both speech and writing more graphic, more interesting, more concrete, and more alive.

Without stopping to think about it, students use figurative language profusely. They pepper their speech with such words as, "He took off like a shot," "He's slow as molasses." Such speech is not only interesting but also vastly more descriptive and graphic than prosaically saying, "He was in a hurry," "He is very slow."

Such descriptive language is in line with Plato's observation that, if we want people to understand us, we must use words that will paint pictures in the minds of our listeners. One can see how much easier it would be to conjure up pictures in one's mind with words "like a shot" and "slow as molasses," than with "hurry" and "slow."

The figurative language, of course, must always be interpreted in the full context of the story. For example, in Thornton Wilder's, *The Bridge of San Luis Rey*, Brother Juniper saw five people plunge into a deep ravine when a primitive rope bridge broke. Wilder described the incident as follows: "he saw the bridge divide and fling five gesticulating ants into the valley below."

In interpreting the above line, one would have to know the context; that is, that this is a moralistic novel and the question of life and death is of paramount importance. So, Brother Juniper, the only witness to the tragedy, is a thoughtful man who undoubtedly reflected that man is frail and tiny and easily killed, like ants.

3. Recognizing Traits of Character

Authors write their stories in such a way that the reader should be able to construct the character of a person along the same lines that he constructs the character of a person in real life; that is, through observing and judging a person's appearance and action, listening to his conversation, as well as hearing the opinions that other people have of him.

The author seldom tells the reader point-blank that a man is courageous. The reader will have to come to such a conclusion himself, reading, for example, an incident in which the person in the story does, in fact, act courageously.

For example, in Erich Remarque's great novel, *All Quiet on the Western Front*, the quality of courage comes through strongly when Paul carries his wounded friend, Kat, on his back to a medical station. What makes the character trait of courage so overwhelming is that Paul risks his own life as he carries Kat across No Man's Land where shells are whistling and exploding and where there is no shelter.

There are other literary devices that an author can use in building up the many facets of a person's character. If the reader is to visualize a full-bodied character, then he must be constantly alert to notice and understand the many subtle cues that the author has carefully and naturally woven into the fabric of the story.

4. Recognizing Tone

When we listen to a speaker, we can tell how he feels toward the subject he is talking about. We can tell whether he is happy or sad, angry or pleased, indifferent or interested, approving or disapproving. We can tell, we say, "by the tone of his voice." Yet, these same states of feeling can be ascertained by reading "silent" words, that is, without hearing an audible voice. Some people are quick to ask, "How can that be?" The answer is that a writer's feelings can be known by his choice of words. For example, it is easy to find out how each of the two writers in the sentences below feels about the same athlete; that is, one likes the athlete, the other dislikes him:

Writer #1:   "He is a rough hulk of a man."
Writer #2:   "He is a veritable bronze giant."

Here is another example. Without hearing his voice, we would have no trouble at all in identifying Winston Churchill's feelings toward Hitler from the following sentence taken from one of his speeches:

Meanwhile Hitler, who had been creeping and worming his way forward, doping and poisoning and pinioning, one after the other Hungary, Rumania and Bulgaria . . .

Invariably, students offer the comment that, upon reading these sentences, they automatically conjure up in their minds a picture of a snake.

If the writing is satirical, it is imperative that the reader ascertain correctly the tone of a writer. The classic satire is Jonathan Swift's "A Modest Proposal," written in 1729. Due to crop failure and general poverty, the Irish people were starving. Swift carefully proposed that the Irish eat their babies. Upon reading this essay some readers were appalled; some thought the idea was drastic, but could save the nation; however, others were sufficiently perceptive to read beyond the words to see that Swift's attitudes were not what the immediate *sense* meanings seemed to suggest.

Swift's *feelings* toward the Irish were feelings of deep sympathy and concern; his *attitude* toward the readers was one of disgust for not crying out at the wrong that brought about such suffering; his *intention* was to shock England into sending food to the Irish to alleviate such suffering. The readers who were able to pick out the satiric tone were able to arrive at the true *sense* meaning, which was different from what it appeared to be on the surface.

Sometimes it is easy to ascertain the tone, sometimes it is difficult; but careful reading and the use of a little imagination will aid the reader in making the correct assessment.

5. Recognizing the Author's Theme or Themes

Being asked to recognize an author's theme or themes in a literary work may sound at first like an overwhelmingly difficult task. But when we convert the general task of finding themes into specific questions, we find that we are on familiar ground. The essential questions that the reader must ask are these: What is the author's subject? What is he driving at? What is his controlling idea? What does the author believe in? What basic stand does he take on this issue? What is his feeling toward life? toward man?

In *Moby Dick,* the central theme deals with man's obsession. Herman Melville shows that the obsession to kill the whale twisted and warped Captain Ahab's personality and judgment so violently that he brought about his own destruction as well as that of innocent men around him.

In Melville's *Moby Dick,* the author develops some secondary themes: (1) he devotes many pages to the beauties and dangers of the sea, describing the scenes vividly so that the reader can better visualize and share the experiences of the whalers; (2) he devotes an entire chapter to explaining and categorizing types of whales to educate the reader in this area; and (3) he deals in many places with moral and ethical problems; for example, in the episode on the flogging of a sailor, Melville makes the point that savages are perhaps not so cruel as civilized people.

In Ernie Pyle's *Brave Men,* he deals mainly with the theme of *courage* as shown by individual soldiers and sailors during the fighting in World War II.

In *The Bridge of San Luis Rey,* Wilder proposes a very lofty, religious theme: the idea of eternity being of first importance to all men, who too seldom reflect on this concept or make best use of their short time on earth.

There is some literature, too, that has no deeper purpose than to provide the reader with a story for enjoyment or escape. Such books are often read for relaxation. As such, they serve a useful purpose; but it would be terribly dull to restrict our reading to literature that never challenges our higher levels of thinking and judging.

6. Recognizing Development of the Theme

While reading literature, the reader must be continually aware of how the author is developing his theme; otherwise, the method will escape notice. Seeing *how* the author put the story together will result in greater understanding. The unaware reader is like an observer who has glimpsed some pieces of cloth laid out on the floor in random positions. He sees the pieces but cannot visualize the finished product. The aware reader, on the other hand, notices the shapes of the pieces, remembers them, and consciously watches the author as he positions and sews them, making up the whole garment. For the aware reader, there are no gaps. The story is full, complete, and well tailored.

Good readers ask questions about the organizational parts of the theme: What important ideas does the author present? Is this an organizational portion of the theme? Why has he placed the parts in this particular order?

If one can first perceive the overall medium or vehicle that the author uses to tell his story, then seeing the parts is made a lot easier. Some of the overall types of novels that influence the development of the theme are historical romance, psychological romance, fictional romance, historical biography, fictional biography, melodrama, moralistic tragedy, realism, adventure, and philosophic study.

HOW TO USE THIS BOOK

We recommend the following sequence of steps:

1. Reread the section entitled "Six Types of Questions." By doing so, you will achieve heightened awareness during the reading of the selections.

2. Read the preface to each selection. You will gain a background of facts and ideas that will aid in the comprehension of the selection.

3. Read the entire selection straight through. By doing so, you will be able to follow more readily the development of the episode and enjoy the story.

4. Answer the six questions at the end of the selection. Indicate your choice by circling the letter (*a, b, c,* or *d*). In answering the questions you may return to the selection to reread it entirely or in part.

1

Mark Twain

(1835-1910)

The Adventures
of Huckleberry Finn

The Adventures of Huckleberry Finn, generally regarded as Mark Twain's greatest work, is a pre-Civil War story of the flight down the Mississippi River of a white boy and a runaway slave. On their large raft equipped with a wigwam and a small canoe, they face problems of navigation, of weather, and of such complications ashore as feuds, murders, and chicaneries.

The river is their source of strength and their avenue of escape from the cruelties and dangers on land. The river is appealing to the lonely boy and the frightened slave, as an escape from all that is wrong in the world.

In this selection from chapter 15, Huck and Jim, the runaway slave, have already been drifting downstream for five nights, having passed Saint Louis, and are now on the wide, swift flowing, island-studded portion of the Mississippi. They are heading for Cairo, Illinois, where they plan to journey northward up the Ohio River to the free states.

At this stage of the trip, we find the pair temporarily separated and lost: Huck has been ashore in his canoe, now he is hurriedly paddling away from shore, trying desperately to find safety with Jim on the raft. The story is told in first person—the voice of Huck.

I throwed the paddle down. I heard the whoop again; it was behind me yet, but in a different place; it kept coming, and kept changing its place, and I kept answering, till by-and-by it was in front of me again and I knowed the current had swung the canoe's head down stream and I was all right, if that was Jim and not some other raftsman hollering. I couldn't tell nothing about voices in a fog, for nothing don't look natural nor sound natural in a fog.

The whooping went on, and in about a minute, I come a booming down on a cut bank with smoky ghosts of big trees on it, and the current throwed me off to the left and shot by, amongst a lot of snags that fairly roared, the current was tearing by them so swift.

In another second or two it was solid white and still again. I set perfectly still, then, listening to my heart thump, and I reckon I didn't draw a breath while it thumped a hundred.

I just give up, then. I knowed what the matter was. That cut bank was an island, and Jim had gone down t'other side of it. It warn't no towhead, that you could float by in ten minutes. It had the big timber of a regular island; it might be five or six mile long and more than a half a mile wide.

I kept quiet, with my ears cocked, about fifteen minutes, I reckon. I was floating along, of course, four or five mile an hour; but you don't ever think of that. No, you *feel* like you are laying dead still on the water; and if a little glimpse of a snag slips by, you don't think to yourself how fast *you're* going, but you catch your breath and think, my! how that snag's tearing along. If you think it ain't dismal and lonesome out in a fog that way, by yourself, in the night, you try it once—you'll see. . . .

Next, for about half an hour, I whoops now and then; at last I hears the answer a long ways off, and tries to follow it, but I couldn't do it, and directly I judged I'd got into a nest of towheads, for I had little dim glimpses of them on both sides of me, sometimes just a narrow channel between; and some that I couldn't see, I knowed was there, because I'd hear the wash of the current against the old dead brush and trash that hung over the banks. Well, I warn't long losing the whoops, down amongst the towheads; and I only tried to chase them a little while, anyway, because it was worse than chasing a Jack-o-lantern. You never knowed a sound dodge around so, and swap places so quick and so much.

I had to claw away from the bank pretty lively, four or five times, to keep from knocking the islands out of the river; and so I judged the raft must be butting into the bank every now and then, or else it would get further ahead and clear out of hearing—it was floating a little faster than what I was.

Well, I seemed to be in the open river again, by-and-by, but I couldn't hear no sign of a whoop nowheres. I reckoned Jim had fetched up on a snag, maybe, and it was all up with him. . . .

It was a monstrous big river here, with the tallest and the thickest kind of timber on both banks; just a solid wall, as well as I could see, by the stars. I looked away down stream, and seen a black speck on the water. I took out after it; but when I got to it it warn't nothing but a couple of saw-logs made fast together. Then I see another speck, and chased that; then another, and this time I was right. It was the raft.

When I got to it, Jim was setting there with his head down between his knees, asleep, with his right arm hanging over the steering oar. The other oar was smashed off, and the raft was littered up with leaves and branches and dirt. So she'd had a rough time.

I made fast and laid down under Jim's nose on the raft, and begun to gap, and stretch my fists out against Jim, and says:

"Hello, Jim, have I been asleep? Why didn't you stir me up?"

"Goodness gracious, is dat you, Huck? En you ain' dead—you ain' drownded—you's back agin? It's too good for true, honey, it's too good for true. Lemme look at you, chile, lemme feel o' you. No, you ain' dead! you's back agin, 'live en soun', jis de same ole Huck—de same ole Huck, thanks to goodness!" . . .

Jim said it made him all over trembly and feverish to be so close to freedom. Well, I can tell you it made me all over trembly and feverish, too, to hear him, because I begun to get it through my head that he *was* most free—and who was to blame for it? Why, *me*. I couldn't get that out of my conscience, no how nor no way. It got to troubling me so I couldn't rest; I couldn't stay still in one place. It hadn't ever come home to me before, what this thing was that I was doing. But now it did; and it staid with me, and scorched me more and more. I tried to make out to myself that I warn't to blame, because I didn't run Jim off from his rightful owner; but it warn't no use, conscience up and says, every time, "But you knowed he was running for his freedom, and you could a paddled ashore and told somebody."

Questions

1. The Adventures of Huckleberry Finn

1. Which is the best of the following definitions of the word *snags* in "a lot of snags that fairly roared, the current was tearing by them so swift"?
   a. trees or stumps
   b. weeds
   c. logs
   d. rocks

2. Which of the following expressions best conveys the meaning of the author's metaphor in "a cut bank with *smoky ghosts* of big trees on it"?
   a. The fog made the trees look smoky.
   b. Huck could barely see the trees in the fog.
   c. Huck was frightened by the trees.
   d. To Huck, the shore represented danger, the river safety.

3. Which of the following character traits is shown by Huckleberry Finn in the selected passage?
   a. discouragement
   b. pessimism
   c. resourcefulness
   d. lack of energy

4. Which of the following definitions best describes the tone of the selected passage?
   a. calm
   b. humorous
   c. sarcastic
   d. anxious

5. Which facet of Mark Twain's philosophy is most strikingly brought out in the selected passage?
   a. All human aspiration is folly.
   b. Happiness comes from temperament not from belief.
   c. Man is fundamentally selfish.
   d. Slavery is an intolerable institution.

6. Which of the following phrases best describes the development of the selection?
   a. a novel of adventure
   b. a moralist's justification of slavery
   c. a description of a phase of American history
   d. an allegorical tale of the river

2

Marjorie Kinnan Rawlings

(1896-1953)

The Yearling

Marjorie Kinnan Rawlings, an American novelist and short-story writer, spent ten years in newspaper work (1918-1928) on the *Louisville Courier-Journal* and the *Rochester* (New York) *Journal* and in writing verse for United Features. In 1928 she purchased an orange grove near Hawthorne, Florida, and devoted her full time to serious writing, drawing upon her friendly contacts and visits with the "Crackers," the poor farmers and hunters of the nearby scrublands. She had great sympathy for these simple people who lived close to starvation, and she wrote convincingly of their folk tales, their customs, and their backwoods speech—all in the vein, not of a reformer, but of an accurate storyteller.

She first attracted national attention with her award-winning short stories: "Jacob's Ladder" (1931) and "Gal Young Un" (1933). In her first full-length novel, *South Moon Under* (1933), she described life in the Florida backwoods in the early 1900s. Her finest book, *The Yearling* (1938), set in the same country thirty years earlier, won her a Pulitzer Prize, election to the National Institute of Arts and Letters (1938), and honorary degrees at Rollins College (1939) and the University of Florida (1941).

Like the juvenile classic *Huckleberry Finn*, *The Yearling* is appreciated as much by adults as by the young for its appealing story of a twelve-year-old boy Jody, his mischievous pet fawn Flag, and his own growing pains. The first section chosen for study from *The Yearling* tells of an apparition that Jody saw on a trip to the sinkhole with Flag. Section 2 shows Pa Baxter's concern lest the yearling fawn eat the young tobacco plants and the corn shoots. Section 3 tells of Jody's reunion with his father after running away in anger when the marauding fawn was destroyed.

I

Ma Baxter said, "This un's too dad-ratted smart," and Penny said, "Why, Ma, shame on you for cussin'," and winked at Jody.

Flag learned to lift the shoe-string latch on the door and come in the house at any hour of the day or night, when he was not shut up. He butted a feather pillow from Jody's bed and tossed it all over the house until it burst, so that feathers drifted for days in every nook and cranny, and appeared from nowhere in a dish of biscuit pudding. He began to romp with the dogs. Old Julia was too dignified to do much more than wag her tail slowly when he pawed at her, but Rip growled and circled and pretended to pounce, and Flag kicked up his heels and flicked his merry tail and shook his head and finally, with impudence, leaped the slat fence and raced alone down the roadway. He liked best to play with Jody. They tussled and held furious butting matches and raced side by side, until Ma Baxter protested that Jody was growing as lean as a black snake.

In a late afternoon toward the end of August, Jody went with the fawn to the sinkhole for fresh water for supper. The road was bright with flowers. The sumac was in bloom, and the colic root sent up tall stalks of white or orange orchid-like flowers. The French mulberries were beginning to ripen on slim stems. They were lavender in color, close-clustered, like snails' eggs along lily stalks. Butterflies sat on the first purple buds of the fragrant deer-tongue, opening and closing their wings slowly, as though waiting for the buds to open and the nectar to be revealed. The covey call of quail sounded again from the pea-field, clear and sweet and communal. Sunset was coming a little earlier, and at the corner of the fence-row, where the old Spanish trail turned north and passed the sinkhole, the saffron light reached under the low-hanging live oaks and made of the gray pendulous Spanish moss a luminous curtain.

Jody stopped short with his hand on the fawn's head. A horseman with a helmet was riding through the moss. Jody took a step forward, and horse and rider vanished, as though their substance were no thicker than the moss. He stepped back and they appeared again. He drew a long breath. Here, certainly, was Fodder-wing's* Spaniard. He was not sure whether he was frightened or no. He was tempted to run back home, telling himself that he had truly seen a spirit. But his father's stuff was in him, and he forced himself to walk forward slowly to the spot in which the apparition had appeared. In a moment the truth was plain. A conjunction of moss and limbs had created the illusion. He could identify the horse, the rider and the

---

*Fodder-wing, a neighbor's son, crippled from birth, and possessing a vivid imagination and story-telling skill, was Jody's best friend.—Ed.

helmet. His heart thumped with relief, yet he was disappointed. It would be better not to have known; to have gone away, believing.

He continued on to the sinkhole. The sweet bay was still in bloom, filling the sinkhole with its fragrance. He longed for Fodder-wing. Now he should never know whether the mossy horseman in the sunset was the Spaniard, or whether Fodder-wing had seen yet another, at once more mystic and more true. He set down his buckets and went down the narrow trail that Penny had cut between banks to the floor of the sinkhole, long before he was born.

He forgot his errand and lay down under the lacy shadow of a dogwood tree at the foot of the slope. The fawn nosed about, then lay down beside him. He could see from this spot the whole deep-sunk bowl at once. The rim above caught the glow of the sunset, as though a ring of fires burned invisibly around it. Squirrels, quieted a moment by his coming, began to bark and chatter and swing across the tree-tops, frenzied with the last hour of day, as they were always frenzied with the first. The palm fronds made a loud rattling.

II

Penny had the furrows open for the corn. Now he went ahead, drilling his holes with a pointed stick down the long rows. Jody followed, dropping two kernels to the hole. He was anxious to please, to have his father forget the shrunken tobacco patch.

He called, "Goes fast, two workin', don't it, Pa?"

Penny did not answer. Yet as the early spring day clouded and the light wind shifted into the southeast and it was plain that a shower would come on the planting, insuring the quick sprouting of the corn, his spirits lifted again. The rain caught them in the late afternoon, but they continued to work and finished the field. It rolled gently, well-tilled and tawny, its soft bosom receptive to the rain. Leaving it, Penny rested on the split-rail fence and looked back over it with satisfaction. There was a wistful look in his eyes as well, as though he were obliged now to leave his handiwork to forces he could only trust blindly not to betray him.

Flag came bounding out of the rain from the south. He came to Jody to be scratched behind the ears. He leaped back and forth in a zig-zag across the fence, then stopped under a mulberry tree and reached up to catch the tip of a bough. Jody sat on the fence beside his father. He turned to call Penny's attention to the slim neck of the fawn stretched up to the new green leaves of the mulberry. His father was studying the young deer with an unfathomable expression. His eyes were narrowed and speculative. He seemed, as when he had set out after old Slewfoot, a stranger. A chill passed over the boy that was not of the dampness of the rain.

He said, "Pa—"

Penny turned to him, startled from his thoughts. He looked down, as though to hide a thing in his eyes.

He said carelessly, "That fawn o' yourn shore growed up in a hurry. He ain't the baby you toted home in your arms all the way that black night— He's a yearlin' now, for shore."

The words gave Jody little pleasure. Somehow, he sensed they were not quite what his father had been thinking. Penny laid his hand an instant on his son's knee.

"You're a pair o' yearlin's," he said. "Hit grieves me."

They slid from the fence and went to the lot to do the chores, then to the house to dry out by the fire. The rain beat lightly on the shingled roof. Flag bleated outside to be allowed to come in. Jody looked appealingly at his mother but she was deaf and blind. Penny felt stiff and sat with his back close to the heat, rubbing his knees. Jody begged some stale cornbread and went outside. He made a fresh bed in the shed and enticed Flag inside with the bread. He sat down and the deer finally doubled his long legs under him and lay down beside him. Jody took hold of the two pointed ears and rubbed his nose against the wet muzzle.

III

Jody said, "How you makin' it, Pa? You better?"

Penny looked a long time into the embers on the hearth.

He said, "You jest as good to know the truth. I ain't scarcely wuth shootin'."

Jody said, "When I git the work done, you got to leave me go fetch ol' Doc to you."

Penny studied him.

He said, "You've done come back different. You've takened a punishment. You ain't a yearlin' no longer. Jody—"

"Yes, sir."

"I'm going to talk to you, man to man. You figgered I went back on you. Now there's a thing ever' man has got to know. Mebbe you know it a'ready. 'Twa'n't only me. 'Twa'n't only your yearlin' deer havin' to be destroyed. Boy, life goes back on you."

Jody looked at his father. He nodded.

Penny said, "You've seed how things goes in the world o' men. You've knowed men to be low-down and mean. You've seed ol' Death at his tricks. You've messed around with ol' Starvation. Ever' man wants life to be a fine thing, and a easy. 'Tis fine, boy, powerful fine, but 'tain't easy. Life knocks a man down and he gits up and it knocks him down agin. I've been uneasy all my life."

His hands worked at the folds of the quilt.

"I've wanted life to be easy for you. Easier'n 'twas for me. A man's heart aches, seein' his young uns face the world. Knowin' they got to git their guts tore out, the way his was tore. I wanted to spare you, long as I could. I wanted you to frolic with your yearlin'. I knowed the lonesomeness he eased for you. But ever' man's lonesome. What's he to do then? What's he to do when he gits knocked down? Why, take it for his share and go on."

Jody said, "I'm 'shamed I runned off."

Penny sat upright.

He said, "You're near enough growed to do your choosin'. Could be you'd crave to go to sea, like Oliver. There's men seems made for the land, and men seems made for the sea. But I'd be proud did you choose to live here and farm the clearin'. I'd be proud to see the day when you got a well dug, so's no woman here'd be obliged to do her washin' on a seepage hillside. You willin'?"

"I'm willin'."

"Shake hands."

He closed his eyes. The fire on the hearth had burned to embers. Jody banked them with the ashes, to assure live coals in the morning.

Penny said, "Now I'll need some he'p, gittin' to the bed. Looks like your Ma's spendin' the night."

Jody put his shoulder under him and Penny leaned heavily on it. He hobbled to his bed. Jody drew the quilt over him.

"Hit's food and drink to have you home, boy. Git to bed and git your rest. 'Night."

The words warmed him through.

" 'Night, Pa."

He went to his room and closed the door. He took off his tattered shirt and breeches and climbed in under the warm quilts. His bed was soft and yielding. He lay luxuriously, stretching his legs. He must be up early in the morning, to milk the cow and bring in wood and work the crops. When he worked them, Flag would not be there to play about with him. His father would no longer take the heavy part of the burden. It did not matter. He could manage alone.

Questions

2. The Yearling

1. What is the best definition of the word *apparition* as used by the author in selection 1?
   a. a spirit
   b. a phantom
   c. a silhouette
   d. an illusion

2. Which of the following expressions best reveals the author's meaning in the personification of *starvation* where Penny says to Jody: "You've messed around with ol' Starvation" (selection 3)?
   a. Jody had been starved for companionship when he took the fawn as a pet.
   b. He had kept Flag even after the fawn had destroyed two plantings of corn.
   c. Jody had nearly starved when he ran away.
   d. He had an intense longing for his parents when he ran away from home.

3. Which of the following character traits of Jody is most forcefully shown in the selections from *The Yearling*?
   a. integrity
   b. laziness
   c. cheerfulness
   d. imagination

4. Which is the best of the following definitions of the tone of the selections from *The Yearling*?
   a. sad
   b. disheartening
   c. sympathetic
   d. cheerful

5. Which of the following phases of the author's philosophy is most clearly revealed in the selections from *The Yearling*?
   a. Kindness is a characteristic quality of people in the backwoods.
   b. A young boy behaves as irresponsibly as a young animal.
   c. As a youth enters his teens he learns to take on responsibility.
   d. Even uneducated, uncultured folk are tolerant of each other.

6. Which of the following best describes the organizational development of *The Yearling*?
   a. a work on a phrase of Florida history
   b. a study of Cracker dialect
   c. a novel of life in the backwoods
   d. a story of a boy growing up

3

Alexandre Dumas

(1802-1870)

The Three Musketeers

Alexandre Dumas *père*, French dramatist and author, wrote *Christine* (1827), *Henry III* (1829), and other romantic dramas that delighted Parisian audiences who until then had been used to classical tragedies. However, he is best known for his prodigious output of historical and romantic novels, many of them being of the "cloak-and-sword" type; the latter group includes *The Three Musketeers* (1844), *The Count of Monte Cristo* (1844), and *The Man in the Iron Mask* (1848) with the action set in France of the early seventeenth century.

His series of Valois novels in which Henry IV is the central character include *Une Fille du Regent* (1845), *La Tulipe Noir* (1850), and *Les Deux Reines* (1864). Other well-known works deal with Mme. du Barry, Marie Antoinette, and events of the French Revolution. His total literary production was 277 volumes!

His son, Alexandre Dumas, *fils* (1824-95), also achieved international fame as a dramatist and author. The latter's play *La Dame aux Camelias* (1848), a phenomenal success, was dignified by the acting of Sarah Bernhardt and Eleanora Duse, and served as a libretto for Verdi's *La Traviata* (1853). A remarkable father and son, the Dumas'!

The selection under study from *The Three Musketeers* covers one set of adventures of the young, swashbuckling D'Artagnan in company with three musketeers of King Louis XIII's guard: the sad Athos, the huge Porthos, and the clever Aramis. These four swordsmen with their four valets (Mousqueton, Bazin, Grimaud, Planchet) have joined to effect the return of Queen Anne's diamond necklace, which she had imprudently given to George Villiers, 1st Duke of Buckingham, now in London. The French

Reprinted from *The Three Musketeers,* by Alexandre Dumas. Used by permission of the publisher, Grosset & Dunlap.

queen's honor is threatened unless she can regain the jewels *within twelve days* to wear at a fete ordered by the king. Cardinal Richelieu and his spies are determined to prevent them from accomplishing their Paris-to-London-and-return mission. Let us examine the fast-paced action.

But at the moment Mousqueton came to announce that the horses were ready, and they were arising from table, the stranger proposed to Porthos to drink the health of the cardinal. Porthos replied that he asked no better, if the stranger, in his turn, would drink the health of the king. The stranger cried that he acknowledged no other king but his Eminence. Porthos called him drunk, and the stranger drew his sword.

"You have committed a piece of folly," said Athos, "but it can't be helped; there is no drawing back. Kill the fellow, and rejoin us as soon as you can."

All three re-mounted their horses, and set out at a good pace, while Porthos was promising his adversary to perforate him with all the thrusts known in the fencing-schools.

"There goes one!" cried Athos, at the end of five hundred paces.

"But why did that man attack Porthos, rather than any other one of us?" asked Aramis.

"Because, as Porthos was talking louder than the rest of us, he took him for the chief," said D'Artagnan.

"I always said that this cadet from Gascony was a well of wisdom," murmured Athos; and the travelers continued their route.

At Beauvais they stopped two hours, as well to breathe their horses a little, as to wait for Porthos. At the end of the two hours, as Porthos did not come, nor any news of him, they resumed their journey.

At a league from Beauvais, where the road was confined between two high banks, they fell in with eight or ten men who, taking advantage of the road being unpaved in this spot, appeared to be employed in digging holes and filling up the ruts with mud.

Aramis, not liking to soil his boots with this artificial mortar, apostrophized them rather sharply. Athos wished to restrain him, but it was too late. The laborers began to jeer the travelers, and by their insolence disturbed the equanimity even of the cool Athos, who urged on his horse against one of them.

Then each of these men retreated as far as the ditch, from which each took a concealed musket; the result was that our seven travelers were outnumbered in weapons. Aramis received a ball which passed through his shoulder, and Mousqueton another ball which lodged in the fleshy part which prolongs the lower portion of the loins. Therefore Mousqueton alone fell from his horse, not because he was severely wounded, but not being able to see the wound, he judged it to be more serious than it really was.

Reading for Ideas

"It is an ambuscade!" shouted D'Artagnan. "Don't waste a charge! Forward!"

Aramis, wounded as he was, seized the mane of his horse, which carried him on with the others. Mousqueton's horse rejoined them, and galloped by the side of his companions.

"That will serve us for a relay," said Athos.

"I would rather have had a hat," said D'Artagnan. "Mine was carried away by a ball. By my faith, it is very fortunate that the letter was not in it."

"They'll kill poor Porthos when he comes up," said Aramis.

"If Porthos were on his legs, he would have rejoined us by this time," said Athos. "My opinion is that on the ground the drunken man was not intoxicated."

They continued at their best speed for two hours, although the horses were so fatigued that it was to be feared they would soon refuse service.

The travelers had chosen cross-roads, in the hope that they might meet with less interruption; but at Crèvecoeur, Aramis declared he could proceed no farther. In fact, it required all the courage which he concealed beneath his elegant form and polished manners to bear him so far. He grew more pale every minute, and they were obliged to support him on his horse. They lifted him off at the door of a cabaret, left Bazin with him, who, besides, in a skirmish was more embarrassing than useful, and set forward again in the hope of sleeping at Amiens.

"*Morbleu,*" said Athos, as soon as they were again in motion, "reduced to two masters and Grimaud and Planchet! *Morbleu!* I won't be their dupe, I will answer for it. I will neither open my mouth, nor draw my sword between this and Calais. I swear by—"

"Don't waste time in swearing," said D'Artagnan; "let us gallop, if our horses will consent."

And the travelers buried their rowels in their horses' flanks, who thus vigorously stimulated recovered their energies. They arrived at Amiens at midnight, and alighted at the *auberge* of the Golden Lily.

The host had the appearance of as honest a man as any on earth. He received the travelers with his candlestick in one hand and his cotton nightcap in the other. He wished to lodge the two travelers each in a charming chamber; but unfortunately these charming chambers were at the opposite extremities of the hôtel. D'Artagnan and Athos refused them. The host replied that he had no other worthy of their Excellencies; but the travelers declared they would sleep in the common chamber, each on a mattress which might be thrown upon the ground. The host insisted but the travelers were firm, and he was obliged to do as they wished.

They had just prepared their beds and barricaded their door within, when some one knocked at the yard-shutter; they demanded who was there, and recognizing the voices of their lackeys, opened the shutter. It was indeed Planchet and Grimaud.

"Grimaud can take care of the horses," said Planchet. "If you are willing, gentlemen, I will sleep across your doorway, and you will then be certain that nobody can reach you."

"And on what will you sleep?" said D'Artagnan.

"Here is my bed," replied Planchet, producing a bundle of straw.

"Come, then," said D'Artagnan, "you are right. Mine host's face does not please me at all; it is too gracious."

"Nor me either," said Athos.

Planchet mounted by the window and installed himself across the doorway, while Grimaud went and shut himself up in the stable, undertaking that by five o'clock in the morning he and the four horses should be ready.

The night was quiet enough. Towards two o'clock in the morning somebody endeavored to open the door; but as Planchet awoke in an instant and cried, "Who goes there?" somebody replied that he was mistaken and went away.

At four o'clock in the morning they heard a terrible riot in the stables. Grimaud had tried to waken the stable-boys, and the stable-boys had beaten him. When they opened the window, they saw the poor lad lying senseless, with his head split by a blow with a pitchfork.

Planchet went down into the yard, and wished to saddle the horses; but the horses were all used up. Mousqueton's horse, which had traveled for five or six hours without a rider the day before, might have been able to pursue the journey; but by an inconceivable error the veterinary surgeon, who had been sent for, as it appeared, to bleed one of the host's horses, had bled Mousqueton's.

This began to be annoying. All these successive accidents were perhaps the result of chance; but they might be the fruits of a plot. Athos and D'Artagnan went out, while Planchet was sent to inquire if there were not three horses for sale in the neighborhood. At the door stood two horses, fresh, strong, and fully equipped. These would just have suited them. He asked where their masters were, and was informed that they had passed the night in the inn, and were then settling their bill with the host.

Athos went down to pay the reckoning, while D'Artagnan and Planchet stood at the street-door. The host was in a lower and back room, to which Athos was requested to go.

Athos entered without the least mistrust, and took out two pistoles to pay the bill. The host was alone, seated before his desk, one of the drawers of which was partly open. He took the money which Athos offered to him, and after turning and turning it over and over in his hands, suddenly cried out that it was bad, and that he would have him and his companions arrested as forgers.

"You blackguard!" cried Athos, going towards him, "I'll cut your ears off!"

At the same instant, four men, armed to the teeth, entered by side-doors, and rushed upon Athos.

"I am taken!" shouted Athos, with all the power of his lungs. "Go on, D'Artagnan! Spur, spur!" and he fired two pistols.

D'Artagnan and Planchet did not require twice bidding; they unfastened the two horses that were waiting at the door, leaped upon them, buried their spurs in their sides, and set off at full gallop.

"Do you know what has become of Athos?" asked D'Artagnan of Planchet, as they galloped on.

"Ah, Monsieur," said Planchet, "I saw one fall at each of his two shots, and he appeared to me, through the glass door, to be fighting with his sword with the others."

"Brave Athos!" murmured D'Artagnan, "and to think that we are compelled to leave him; maybe the same fate awaits us two paces hence. Forward, Planchet, forward! you are a brave fellow."

"As I told you, Monsieur," replied Planchet, "Picards are found out by being used. Besides, I am here in my own country, and that excites me."

And both, with free use of the spur, arrived at St. Omer without drawing a bit. At St. Omer they breathed their horses with the bridles passed under their arms for fear of accident, and ate a morsel from their hands on the stones of the street, after which they departed again.

At a hundred paces from the gates of Calais, D'Artagnan's horse gave out, and could not by any means be made to get up again, the blood flowing from his eyes and his nose. There still remained Planchet's horse; but he stopped short, and could not be made to move a step.

Fortunately, as we have said, they were within a hundred paces of the city; they left their two nags upon the highroad, and ran towards the quay. Planchet called his master's attention to a gentleman who had just arrived with his lackey, and only preceded them by about fifty paces. They made all speed to come up to this gentleman, who appeared to be in great haste. His boots were covered with dust, and he inquired if he could not instantly cross over to England.

"Nothing would be more easy," said the captain of a vessel ready to set sail, "but this morning came an order to let no one leave without express permission from the cardinal."

"I have that permission," said the gentleman, drawing a paper from his pocket; "here it is."

"Have it examined by the governor of the port," said the ship-master, "and give me the preference."

"Where shall I find the governor?"

"At his country-house."

"And that is situated?"

"At a quarter of a league from the city. Look, you may see it from here—at the foot of that little hill, that slated roof."

"Very well," said the gentleman. And, with his lackey, he took the road to the governor's country-house.

D'Artagnan and Planchet followed the gentleman at a distance of five hundred paces. Once outside the city, D'Artagnan overtook the gentleman as he was entering a little wood.

"Monsieur," said D'Artagnan, "you appear to be in great haste?"

"No one can be more so, Monsieur."

Questions

3. The Three Musketeers

1. In the episode in which eight or ten men appeared to be employed in digging holes and filling up the ruts with mud, which of the expressions listed below explains the word *apostrophized* as used in the following sentence: "Aramis, not liking to soil his boots with this artificial mortar, apostrophized them rather sharply"?

   a. He digressed from his talk.
   b. He upbraided the men.
   c. He criticized the men.
   d. He expostulated.

2. When Dumas wrote that D'Artagnan and his valet, Planchet, "ate a morsel from their hands on the stones of the street," what did the author mean by alluding to the stones of the street?

   a. The two men sat on the stones.
   b. They spread their meal on the stones.
   c. The hardships they faced are compared to the hardness of stones.
   d. They were in too much of a hurry to go to an inn and ate standing in the street.

3. Which of D'Artagnan's traits of character is most forcefully brought out in the selection?
   a. leadership
   b. canniness
   c. self-confidence
   d. bravery

4. Which of the following terms best applies to the tone of the selection from *The Three Musketeers*?
   a. serious and logical
   b. emotive and personal
   c. figurative or symbolic
   d. moralistic or doctrinal

5. Which of the following statements best explains Dumas' philosophy as shown in the selection from *The Three Musketeers*?
   a. A worthy goal is reason enough for risking one's life.
   b. In times of trouble, place no confidence in strangers.
   c. In armed conflict, men need a capable leader.
   d. Faithful companions inspire in each other a binding spirit of courage and unselfish devotion.

6. Which of the following expressions best describes the pattern of development of the selected passage?
   a. a mystery story
   b. an argument against violence
   c. a historical romance
   d. a novel of intrigue

4

John Hersey

(1914-   )

A Bell for Adano

John Hersey, a journalist and novelist, was born of American parents in Tienstin, China, June 17, 1914. When his family returned to the United States, he attended the Hotchkiss School 1927-32, then Yale University where he received the B.A. degree in 1936.

After spending the year 1936-37 at Clare College of Cambridge University in England, he served as private secretary to Sinclair Lewis the following summer. Then he began a career as a writer for, and later an editor of, three magazines: *Time, Life*, and the *New Yorker*.

Of his thirteen works, from *Men on Bataan* (1932) to *Under the Eye of the Storm* (1967), his best known is *A Bell for Adano* (1944), for which he received the Pulitzer Prize in 1945. He is a member of the American Academy of Arts and Letters and of the Authors' League of America, and is now Master of Pierson College at Yale.

A Bell for Adano is a fictionalized account of the administration of Major Victor Joppolo as head officer of the Allied Military Government Occupied Territory in Adano, Italy, in 1943 during World War II. Since Joppolo is himself an Italian-American, he treats the impoverished, war-weary citizens of Adano with understanding. He restores their fishing privileges, works to reestablish the life of the village, and wins the enthusiastic acclaim of the townspeople by obtaining a large bronze bell to replace the one earlier melted down by the Italians for munitions.

The first section tells of the need for permitting the use of carts, and of Major Joppolo's order countermanding General Marvin's decision to prohibit them. Section 2 reveals the loneliness of army men overseas. Section 3 gives an account of Joppolo's speech at the installation of the bell in the clock tower, and of General Marvin's order for the major's transfer out of the town he had served so well.

I

". . . mine was a cart for food, to make other people fat and jovial, though they might have a certain amount of hard breathing."

The Major said: "This is a waste of time." But Basile could see, and the other two could see, that the Major was nearly persuaded by this time-wasting talk.

Basile pressed on: "How can I drive my cart now, even in the country? How can I put my fat horse, whose name is General Eisenhower in honor of our deliverer, between the shafts, and put my fat self on the seat, and drive around with my pictures of fat and holy people—when the people of Adano are starving, Mister Major? This fills me with shame, even though I cannot bring the cart into town."

And then, with great craft, Basile said: "There is nothing in all the proclamations, even though it takes you a week to read them, which says that the Americans came to Adano in order to make people die of hunger. And there is nothing in all the proclamations which refers to such things as the dead mule of Errante Gaetano. Why then do we have this thing of the carts?"

The Major said to himself in English: "Damn."

He reached for the field telephone, cranked the handle, and said: "Give me Rowboat Blue Forward."

While he waited for an answer, the Major said to Basile gruffly: "Sit down."

"Hello. This Rowboat Blue Forward? Captain Purvis, please. . . .

"Purvis? Joppolo. Listen. . . .

"No, now this is serious, Purvis. This thing about the carts. I've made up my mind. By one sentence General Marvin destroyed the work of nine days in this town. I know it may mean a court martial, but I've decided to countermand his order. What? . . .

"I know I'm taking a hell of a chance, but I've got to do it. We can't let these people starve. . . .

"I have to do it, Purvis. This town is dying. No food can get into the town if the carts don't come. The town depends on the carts for water: there isn't any running water here, you know that. The people can't go out into the fields to work in the morning. Taking carts away from this town is like taking automobiles away from a country town in the States. You just can't do it all at once. People will die. I'm not here to kill people."

Captain Purvis evidently put up an argument.

Finally the Major said: "Purvis, I order you, on my authority, to start letting carts back into the town, beginning now. I take absolute and complete responsiblity for countermanding General Marvin's order. . . .

"Listen friend, if we never took chances around here, this place would go right on being a Fascism. All right, the hell with you, it's on my responsibility."

The three cartmen sat through the telephone conversation not comprehending. To judge by their faces they seemed to think that Major Joppolo was devising some punishment for them. They had the habit of fear, and they thought that this man of authority would of course be exactly like the men of authority they had known for so long.

Major Joppolo hung up. He turned to the three cartmen and said: "You may bring your carts into the town."

For a long moment they did not understand. Then they stood up and began shouting and waving their caps.

"We thank you, we thank you and we kiss your hand," they roared.

"Oh, Mister Major, there has never been a thing like this," the fat one named Basile shouted, "that the poor should come to the Palazzo di Città, and that their request should be granted."

"Especially," shouted the loud one named Afronti, "especially without a wait of two to three weeks."

II

"Where is Florida?"

"It's in the south, I wasn't there at all. That was the second time I lied to get a job. Since then I've tried never to lie, the truth is much better and much safer. So they gave me a job in the Sanitation Department. Later I took my examinations for advancement to Third Class Clerk, and afterwards I got to be a Second Class Clerk. I was earning forty-two dollars a week when I went into the Army." Major Joppolo was getting a little boastful about his non-existent riches. "That was four thousand two hundred lira a week."

Tina said: "The wife, is she pretty?"

Major Joppolo said: "Yes, she is very pretty, at least she seems so to me. I miss her very much. She has a mole on the left side of her chin, but otherwise she is very pretty. She is of Italian parentage, so she has dark skin like yours. In some ways you remind me of her."

Tina had been looking up at the stars. But now she suddenly looked down into the dark valley of the street and said: "Let's go in and dance." And she opened up the shutter doors and went inside. Major Joppolo went in after her.

Captain Purvis had gone to work on Tomasino's wine, and he was making a decided nuisance of himself, so Major Joppolo persuaded him to go home. He and Giuseppe led the Captain home.

When he got back to his own villa, and was undressed and in bed, Major Joppolo felt miserable. It wasn't until nearly three o'clock that he realized why. Giuseppe was right. It made a man feel very unhappy to be as far from home as the Bronx, New York, is from Adano, Italy.

The next morning Captain Purvis sat with his feet up on his desk. He was in a bad humor.

Sergeant Trapani was out of the office. The Captain spoke to Corporal Chuck Schultz, who was on guard. "That Major Joppolo," he said. "I was beginning to like him, but he's a wet blanket. God, I was just getting a wonderful buzz on last night, and he descended on me, sober as a whitefish, and he made me go home."

Corporal Schultz said: "Was you getting buzzed on that Dago red?"

The Captain said: "Yeah, there's an old fish-hound down there. Giuseppe took me to his house because he's got a couple of nice quail, he gave me some red stuff."

The Corporal said: "That *vino's* murder, Captain. . . .

III

. . . thoughts began to sort themselves out, and everything came very straight to Major Joppolo.

He would say a few words, he thought, about the removal of the old bell. Then he would tell about how the people of Adano had interested him in trying to get a new one. Then a few words about Corelli, and what he had done for Italians in the last war, and then the meaning today of the inscription on the bell, *America ed Italia,* America and Italy, and then perhaps something about the Americans' Liberty Bell. After talking about it that day, the Major had been curious about the Liberty Bell, and he had written a letter back to Amgot headquarters inquiring about it, and now he would be able to explain the crack, and he would tell the people of Adano the inscription on that bell, the words from Leviticus: "Proclaim liberty throughout the land and to all the inhabitants thereof."

And then everything was wonderfully clear in the mind of Victor Joppolo. He knew exactly what he would say. Words came to him which were beautiful and were the truth about the new bell and its meaning for Adano, and about what he, Victor Joppolo, wanted for the people of Adano. The words were as clear as anything can be, and as true.

At about two o'clock the courier came by motorcycle from Vicinamare. From his office Sergeant Borth saw him throw the pouch onto the sidewalk in front of the Palazzo. Mail, even official mail, was enough of an event so that Sergeant Borth got up and went across to the Palazzo and up to Major Joppolo's office to see what there was.

In time he came on a paper addressed to Major Joppolo. He read it:

"*1. You are authorized to proceed by first available transportation to A.F.H.Q., Algiers, via port of Vicinamare.*

"*2. Reassignment of station will be made by A.F.H.Q.*

"*3. Reason for this order is that reference (1) did wilfully and without consultation countermand orders issued by General Marvin, 49th Division, re entry of mule carts into town of Adano."*

And the order was signed by General Marvin.

Sergeant Borth folded the order, put it in his pocket, and left the building. He went directly to the M.P. command post in the Fascio.

He said to Captain Purvis: "The Major's been relieved."

Captain Purvis said: "What the hell do you mean?"

"Just what I said: he's been ordered back to Algiers for reassignment."

"What the hell for?"

"Insubordination. Countermanding an order by Marvin about mule carts. I guess it was after that affair of the mule the General shot outside town."

Captain Purvis had forgotten all about the report he had sent to Division. Now that he remembered he didn't have the courage to say anything about it. All he said was: "What a hell of a note."

Borth said: "I'll say it's a hell of a note. The Major's just begun to accomplish things in this town."

Questions

4. A Bell for Adano

1. Which of the following best reveals the meaning of the word *countermand* used in the following sentence: "I've decided to countermand his order"?
   a. to rewrite the order in plain language
   b. to issue an alternative order
   c. to issue an equivalent order
   d. to revoke or cancel the former order

2. Which of the following is the best explanation of the author's intention when he has Major Joppolo declare: "'Taking carts away from this town is like taking automobiles from a country town in the States'"?
   a. Transportation of commodities is hampered.
   b. Social calls and events are curtailed.
   c. Pleasure trips are stopped.
   d. The whole economy breaks down.

3. Which of Major Joppolo's traits of character is most clearly shown in the selections from *A Bell for Adano*?
   a. truthfulness
   b. vision
   c. aggressiveness
   d. daring

4. Which of the following words best defines the tone of the passages selected from *A Bell for Adano*?
   a. critical
   b. ironic
   c. sympathetic
   d. hopeful

5. Which of the following statements best reveals the author's philosophy?
   a. Government is effective when its administration is based upon justice and consideration for the needs of the people.
   b. People need a symbol of liberty.
   c. People respond favorably to just treatment.
   d. People recognize a capable administrator.

6. Which of the following phrases best illustrates the organizational development of *A Bell for Adano*?
   a. a historical novel
   b. a wartime story
   c. a sympathetic social study
   d. a tale of military government

5

Charlotte Brontë

(1816-1855)

Jane Eyre

The novel *Jane Eyre* exhibits some similarities to its author's life. The Jane of the novel is an orphan who is penniless yet self-reliant and studious; she becomes a governess, a teacher, and finally the wife of the man she loves. Charlotte Brontë, the author, in her short life of thirty-nine years, lost her mother at an early age, cared for her ailing, blind father, bore the sorrow of the death of her four sisters and her only brother, and finally married just one year before her death.

Jane in the novel survived deprivation and cruelty at boarding school and dependence and poverty as a governess. Charlotte, the author, valiantly survived the miseries of her year in the harsh discipline and physical discomfort of a badly run boarding school and the constant strain of being a governess in other people's homes.

In *Jane Eyre* Miss Brontë introduced a type of heroine new to British literature—a heroine poor and plain like herself but endowed with the initiative and capability usually reserved for masculine characters of the fiction of that era.

The first reprinted section covers a conversation between Jane (age ten) and her aunt Mrs. Reed. Section 2 presents Jane as a young woman serving as a governess in the home of Mr. Edward Rochester. In section 3 Jane returns to Mr. Rochester, now a widower, maimed, and almost totally blind.

Reprinted from *Jane Eyre*, by Charlotte Brontë. Used by permission of the publisher, Harper & Brothers.

I

With these words, Mr. Brocklehurst put into my hand a thin pamphlet sewn in a cover, and having rung for his carriage, he departed.

Mrs. Reed and I were left alone: some minutes passed in silence; she was sewing, I was watching her. Mrs. Reed might be at that time some six or seven and thirty; she was a woman of robust frame, square-shouldered and strong-limbed, not tall, and, though stout, not obese: she had a somewhat large face, the under-jaw being much developed and very solid; her brow was low, her chin large and prominent, mouth and nose sufficiently regular; under her light eyebrows glimmered an eye devoid of ruth; her skin was dark and opaque, her hair nearly flaxen; her constitution was sound as a bell—illness never came near her; she was an exact, clever manager, her household and tenantry were thoroughly under her control; her children, only, at times defied her authority, and laughed it to scorn; she dressed well, and had a presence and port calculated to set off handsome attire.

Sitting on a low stool, a few yards from her arm-chair, I examined her figure; I perused her features. In my hand I held the tract, containing the sudden death of the Liar: to which narrative my attention had been pointed as to an appropriate warning. What had just passed; what Mrs. Reed had said concerning me to Mr. Brocklehurst; the whole tenor of their conversation, was recent, raw, and stinging in my mind; I had felt every word as acutely as I had heard it plainly, and a passion of resentment fomented now within me.

Mrs. Reed looked up from her work; her eye settled on mine, her fingers at the same time suspended their nimble movements.

"Go out of the room; return to the nursery," was her mandate. My look or something else must have struck her as offensive, for she spoke with extreme, though suppressed irritation. I got up, I went to the door; I came back again; I walked to the window, across the room, then close up to her.

Speak I must: I had been trodden on severely, and *must* turn: but how? What strength had I to dart retaliation at my antagonist? I gathered my energies and launched them in this blunt sentence:—

"I am not deceitful: if I were, I should say I loved *you*; but I declare I do not love you: I dislike you the worst of anybody in the world except John Reed; and this book about the liar, you may give to your girl, Georgiana, for it is she who tells lies, and not I."

Mrs. Reed's hands still lay on her work inactive: her eye of ice continued to dwell freezingly on mine.

"What more have you to say?" she asked, rather in the tone in which a person might address an opponent of adult age than such as is ordinarily used to a child.

That eye of hers, that voice stirred every antipathy I had. Shaking from head to foot, thrilled with ungovernable excitement, I continued:—

"I am glad you are no relation of mine: I will never call you aunt again as long as I live. I will never come to see you when I am grown up; and if any one asks me how I liked you, and how you treated me, I will say the very thought of you makes me sick, and that you treated me with miserable cruelty."

"How dare you affirm that, Jane Eyre?"

"How dare I, Mrs. Reed? How dare I? Because it is the *truth*. You think I have no feelings, and that I can do without one bit of love or kindness; but I cannot live so: and you have no pity. I shall remember how you thrust me back—roughly and violently thrust me back—into the red-room, and locked me up there, to my dying day; though I was in agony; though I cried out, while suffocating with distress, 'Have mercy! have mercy, aunt Reed!' And that punishment you made me suffer because your wicked boy struck me—knocked me down for nothing. I will tell anybody who asks me questions, this exact tale. People think you a good woman, but you are bad; hard-hearted. *You* are deceitful!"

Ere I had finished this reply, my soul began to expand, to exult, with the strangest sense of freedom, of triumph, I ever felt. It seemed as if an invisible bond had burst, and that I had struggled out into unhoped-for liberty. Not without cause was this sentiment: Mrs. Reed looked frightened; her work had slipped from her knee; she was lifting up her hands, rocking herself to and fro, and even twisting her face as if she would cry.

"Jane, you are under a mistake: what is the matter with you? Why do you tremble so violently? Would you like to drink some water?"

II

I grieved for his grief, whatever that was, and would have given much to assuage it.

Though I had now extinguished my candle and was laid down in bed, I could not sleep, for thinking of his look when he paused in the avenue, and told how his destiny had risen up before him, and dared him to be happy at Thornfield.

"Why not?" I asked myself. "What alienates him from the house? Will he leave it again soon? Mrs. Fairfax said he seldom stayed here longer than a fortnight at a time; and he has now been resident eight weeks. If he does go, the change will be doleful. Suppose he should be absent, spring, summer, and autumn: how joyless sunshine and fine days will seem!"

I hardly know whether I had slept or not after this musing; at any rate, I started wide awake on hearing a vague murmur, peculiar and lugubrious, which sounded, I thought, just above me. I wished I had kept my candle burning: the night was drearily dark; my spirits were depressed. I rose and sat up in bed, listening. The sound was hushed.

I tried again to sleep; but my heart beat anxiously: my inward tranquillity was broken. The clock, far down in the hall, struck two. Just then it seemed my chamber-door was touched; as if fingers had swept the panels in groping a way along the dark gallery outside. I said, "Who is there?" Nothing answered. I was chilled with fear.

All at once I remembered that it might be Pilot: who, when the kitchen-door chanced to be left open, not unfrequently found his way up to the threshold of Mr. Rochester's chamber: I had seen him lying there myself, in the mornings. The idea calmed me somewhat: I lay down. Silence composes the nerves; and as an unbroken hush now reigned again through the whole house, I began to feel the return of slumber. But it was not fated that I should sleep that night. A dream had scarcely approached my ear, when it fled affrighted, scared by a marrow-freezing incident enough.

This was a demoniac laugh—low, suppressed, and deep—uttered, as it seemed, at the very key-hole of my chamber door. The head of my bed was near the door, and I thought at first the goblin-laughter stood at my bedside—or rather, crouched, by my pillow: but I rose, looked round, and could see nothing; while, as I still gazed, the unnatural sound was reiterated: and I knew it came from behind the panels. My first impulse was to rise and fasten the bolt; my next, again to cry out, "Who is there?"

Something gurgled and moaned. Ere long, steps retreated up the gallery towards the third story staircase: a door had lately been made to shut in that staircase; I heard it open and close, and all was still.

"Was that Grace Poole? and is she possessed with a devil?" thought I. Impossible now to remain longer by myself: I must go to Mrs. Fairfax. I hurried on my frock and a shawl; I withdrew the bolt and opened the door with a trembling hand. There was a candle burning just outside, left on the matting in the gallery. I was surprised at this circumstance: but still more was I amazed to perceive the air quite dim, as if filled with smoke; and, while looking to the right hand and left, to find whence these blue wreaths issued, I became further aware of a strong smell of burning.

Something creaked: it was a door ajar, and that door was Mr. Rochester's, and the smoke rushed in a cloud from thence. I thought no more of Mrs. Fairfax; I thought no more of Grace Poole or the laugh: in an instant, I was within the chamber. Tongues of flame darted round the bed: the curtains were on fire. In the midst of blaze and vapour, Mr. Rochester lay stretched motionless, in deep sleep.

"Wake! wake!" I cried—I shook him, but he only murmured and turned: the smoke had stupefied him. Not a moment could be lost: the very sheets were kindling. I rushed to his basin and ewer; fortunately, one was wide and the other deep, and both were filled with water. I heaved them up, deluged the bed and its occupant, flew back to my own room, brought my own water-jug, baptized the couch afresh, and, by God's aid succeeded in extinguishing the flames which were devouring it.

The hiss of the quenched element, the breakage of a pitcher which I had flung from my hand when I had emptied it, and, above all, the splash of the shower-bath I had liberally bestowed, roused Mr. Rochester at last. Though it was now dark, I knew he was awake; because I heard him fulminating strange anathemas at finding himself lying in a pool of water.

III

"I have little left in myself—I must have you. The world may laugh—may call me absurd, selfish—but it does not signify. My very soul demands you: it will be satisfied: or it will take deadly vengeance on its frame."

"Well, sir, I will stay with you: I have said so."

"Yes—but you understand one thing by staying with me: and I understand another. You, perhaps, could make up your mind to be about my hand and chair—to wait on me as a kind of little nurse (for you have an affectionate heart and a generous spirit, which prompt you to make sacrifices for those you pity) and that ought to suffice for me no doubt. I suppose I should now entertain none but fatherly feeling for you: do you think so? Come—tell me."

"I will think what you like, sir: I am content to be only your nurse, if you think it better."

"But you cannot always be my nurse, Jane: you are young—you must marry one day."

"I don't care about being married."

"You should care, Jane: if I were what I once was, I would try to make you care—but—a sightless block!"

He relapsed again into gloom. I, on the contrary, became more cheerful, and took fresh courage: these last words gave me an insight as to where the difficulty lay; and as it was no difficulty with me, I felt quite relieved from my previous embarrassment. I resumed a livelier vein of conversation.

"It is time some one undertook to rehumanize you," said I, parting his thick and long uncut locks; "for I see you are being metamorphosed into a lion, or something of that sort. You have a 'faux air' of Nebuchadnezzar in the fields about you, that is certain: your hair reminds me of eagles' feathers; whether your nails are grown like birds' claws or not, I have not yet noticed."

"On this arm, I have neither hand nor nails," he said, drawing the mutilated limb from his breast, and showing it to me. "It is a mere stump—a ghastly sight! Don't you think so, Jane?"

"It is a pity to see it; and a pity to see your eyes—and the scar of fire on your forehead: and the worst of it is, one is in danger of loving you too well for all this; and making too much of you."

"I thought you would be revolted, Jane, when you saw my arm, and my cicatrized visage."

"Did you? Don't tell me so—lest I should say something disparaging to your judgment. Now, let me leave you an instant, to make a better fire, and have the hearth swept up. Can you tell when there is a good fire?"

"Yes; with the right eye I see a glow—a ruddy haze."

"And you see the candles?"

"Very dimly—each is a luminous cloud."

"Can you see me?"

"No, my fairy: but I am only too thankful to hear and feel you."

"When do you take supper?"

"I never take supper."

"But you shall have some to-night. I am hungry: so are you, I daresay, only you forget."

Summoning Mary, I soon had the room in more cheerful order: I prepared him, likewise, a comfortable repast. My spirits were excited, and with pleasure and ease I talked to him during supper, and for a long time after. There was no harassing restraint, no repressing of glee and vivacity with him; for with him I was at perfect ease, because I knew I suited him: all I said or did seemed either to console or revive him. Delightful consciousness! It brought to life and light my whole nature: in his presence I thoroughly lived; and he lived in mine. Blind as he was smiles played over his face, joy dawned on his forehead: his lineaments softened and warmed.

After supper, he began to ask me many questions, of where I had been, what I had been doing, how I have found him out; but I gave him only very partial replies: it was too late to enter into particulars that night. Besides, I wished to touch no deep-thrilling chord—to open no fresh well of emotion in his heart: my sole present aim was to cheer him. Cheered, as I have said, he was: and yet but by fits. If a moment's silence broke the conversation, he would turn restless, touch me, then say, "Jane."

"You are altogether a human being, Jane? You are certain of that?"

"I conscientiously believe so, Mr. Rochester."

"Yet how, on this dark and doleful evening, could you so suddenly rise on my lone hearth? I stretched my hand to take a glass of water from a hireling, and it was given me by you: I asked a question, expecting John's wife to answer me, and your voice spoke in my ear."

"Because I had come in, in Mary's stead, with the tray."

Questions

5. Jane Eyre

1. Which of the following expressions best indicates what the author had in mind when using the word *cicatrized* in Mr. Rochester's statement: " 'I thought you would be revolted, Jane, when you saw my arm, and my cicatrized visage' "?
   a. Mr. Rochester's face had been seriously burned.
   b. His face was contorted from suffering.
   c. New scar tissue now covered the damaged area.
   d. His face had been operated on.

2. Which of the following statements best explains Jane's meaning when she declares to Mr. Rochester, " 'It is time someone undertook to rehumanize you' "?
   a. He needs to be remade in every way.
   b. He is careless of his appearance.
   c. He is moody.
   d. He is gloomy.

3. Which of the following character traits of Jane is most strikingly shown in the selections from *Jane Eyre*?
   a. honesty
   b. reverence
   c. self-reliance
   d. passion

4. Which of the following best describes the tone of the passages selected from *Jane Eyre*?
   a. despondent
   b. foreboding
   c. hopeful
   d. serious

5. Which of the following statements best illustrates Charlotte Brontë's philosophy?
   a. Every person is a force for good or evil.
   b. The author is a Puritan.
   c. The author respects plainness in people.
   d. The author believes in the initiative and independence of women.

6. Which of the following best describes the organizational development of *Jane Eyre*?
   a. a historical novel
   b. a psychological romance with the heroine as the narrator
   c. a melodramatic story
   d. a mystery

6

Edgar Allan Poe

(1809-1849)

The Gold Bug

Edgar Allan Poe in his prose work produced tales of mystery such as "The Gold Bug" and "The Purloined Letter," and tales of horror such as "The Pit and the Pendulum" and "The Cask of Amontillado," and also tales intended both to mystify and shock the reader as in *The Murders in the Rue Morgue.* His power of inventiveness and his ability to sustain suspense are most strikingly exemplified in "The Gold Bug," notable for the many complicated calculations and deductions following the discovery of a pirate's treasure-trove map. The story is told in the first person with the narrator so puzzled by Legrand's fascination for the gold bug that he believes his friend to be verging on madness until the latter actually finds the treasure and then explains the ingenious reasoning (comparable to that of Sherlock Holmes) that pointed step by step to the solution. In fact, the completeness of Poe's explanation coupled with the tale's mystery and suspense establish "The Gold Bug" as a masterpiece of detective fiction. (Poe has been called the inventor of the detective story.) The selection here presented for analysis starts at the point where Legrand is telling Jupiter how to drop the gold bug as, it turns out later, the pirate's map directed.

"Is de lef eye of de skull pon de same side as de lef hand of de skull too?—cause de skull aint got not a bit ob a hand at all—nebber mind! I got de lef eye now—here de lef eye! what mus do wid it?"

Reprinted from "The Gold Bug," by Edgar Allan Poe, *The Works of Poe,* Reprinted by permission of the publisher, Walter J. Black, Inc.

"Let the beetle drop through it, as far as the string will reach—but be careful and not let go your hold of the string."

"All dat done, Massa Will; mighty easy ting for to put de bug fru de hole—look out for him dare below!"

During this colloquy no portion of Jupiter's person could be seen; but the beetle, which he had suffered to descend, was now visible at the end of the string, and glistened, like a globe of burnished gold, in the last rays of the setting sun, some of which still faintly illumined the eminence upon which we stood. The *scarabaeus* hung; quite clear of any branches, and, if allowed to fall, would have fallen at our feet. Legrand immediately took the scythe, and cleared with it a circular space, three or four yards in diameter, just beneath the insect, and, having accomplished this, ordered Jupiter to let go the string and come down from the tree.

Driving a peg, with great nicety, into the ground, at the precise spot where the beetle fell, my friend now produced from his pocket a tape-measure. Fastening one end of this at that point of the trunk of the tree which was nearest the peg, he unrolled it till it reached the peg and thence further unrolled it, in the direction already established by the two points of the tree and the peg, for the distance of fifty feet—Jupiter clearing away the brambles with the scythe. At the spot thus attained a second peg was driven, and about this, as a center, a rude circle, about four feet in diameter, described. Taking now a spade himself, and giving one to Jupiter and one to me, Legrand begged us to set about digging as quickly as possible.

To speak the truth, I had no especial relish for such amusement at any time, and, at that particular moment, would willingly have declined it; for the night was coming on, and I felt much fatigued with the exercise already taken; but I saw no mode of escape, and was fearful of disturbing my poor friend's equanimity by a refusal. Could I have depended, indeed upon Jupiter's aid, I would have had no hesitation in attempting to get the lunatic home by force; but I was too well assured of the old Negro's disposition, to hope that he would assist me, under any circumstances, in a personal contest with his master. I made no doubt that the latter had been infected with some of the innumerable Southern superstitions about money buried, and that his phantasy had received confirmation by the finding of the *scarabaeus*, or, perhaps, by Jupiter's obstinacy in maintaining it to be "a bug of real gold." A mind disposed to lunacy would readily be led away by such suggestions—especially if chiming in with favorite preconceived ideas—and then I called to mind the poor fellow's speech about the beetle's being "the index of his fortune." Upon the whole, I was sadly vexed and puzzled, but, at length, I concluded to make a virtue of necessity—to dig with a good will, and thus the sooner to convince the visionary, by ocular demonstration, of the fallacy of the opinion he entertained.

The lanterns having been lit, we all fell to work with a zeal worthy a more rational cause; and, as the glare fell upon our persons and implements, I could not help thinking how picturesque a group we composed, and how

Reading for Ideas

strange and suspicious our labors must have appeared to any interloper who, by chance, might have stumbled upon our whereabouts.

We dug very steadily for two hours. Little was said; and our chief embarrassment lay in the yelpings of the dog, who took exceeding interest in our proceedings. He, at length, became so obstreperous that we grew fearful of his giving the alarm to some stragglers in the vicinity—or, rather, this was the apprehension of Legrand;—for myself, I should have rejoiced at any interruption which might have enabled me to get the wanderer home.

Questions

6. The Gold Bug

1. Which of the following definitions best conveys Poe's idea in using the word *scarabaeus*?
   a. a faience beetle
   b. a talisman
   c. a live beetle
   d. a beetle made of stone

2. Which of the following phrases expresses the meaning of the simile "like a globe of burnished gold" as applied to the beetle "at the end of the string"?
   a. like an inanimate sphere
   b. like a reflection of the setting sun
   c. like a beacon of hope
   d. like a last spark before nightfall

3. Which of the following is the most noticeable character trait of Legrand from the context of the selection from "The Gold Bug"?
   a. He was superstitious.
   b. He was mentally upset.
   c. He was determined.
   d. He was insane.

4. Which of the following best describes the tone of the passage selected from "The Gold Bug"?

   a. a sense of fear in the presence of a man seemingly unbalanced
   b. an effect of frustration
   c. a feeling of impending disaster
   d. an atmosphere of mystery and suspense

5. Which one of the following expressions is *not* in line with Poe's philosophy as revealed in the selected passage?

   a. Wrong conclusions proceed from insufficient evidence.
   b. Queer conduct is easily misconstrued.
   c. Life's puzzles can be solved by some men, not by others.
   d. Avarice can lead to mental derangement.

6. Which of the following phrases best describes the pattern of development?

   a. a story of mystery and horror
   b. a story of mystery and analysis
   c. a pathological study
   d. a story of mystery and dangerous situations

7

Robert Louis Stevenson

(1850-1894)

Treasure Island

Robert Louis Stevenson was born in 1850, in Scotland. Ill much of his life, he traveled widely in France, Switzerland, the United States, and finally to the South Seas, in search of a climate that would be beneficial to his health. He finally settled in Samoa, where he died of tuberculosis at the age of forty-four.

His principal works are *Treasure Island* (1883), one of the most beloved adventure stories ever written; *A Child's Garden of Verses* (1885), in which the spirit of the frail, sensitive, eager, young Robert Louis Stevenson still lives; *The Strange Case of Dr. Jekyll and Mr. Hyde* (1886), names that have entered the language to signify a horrifyingly split personality; and *Kidnapped* (1886) and *The Master of Ballantrae* (1889), adventure stories.

Treasure Island is an adventure romance of the 1740s, set in England and the Spanish Main. The principal characters are Jim Hawkins, cabin boy of the *Hispaniola*; Dr. Livesey, a friend of Jim's; Squire Trelawney, a wealthy landowner; Mr. Smollett, captain of the *Hispaniola*; Long John Silver, leader of the mutineers; and Ben Gunn, a long-marooned pirate.

The first section tells how Jim repulsed the mutineer, Mr. Hands, after taking possession of the ship; section 2 covers a tense interview between Jim and Long John Silver; in section 3 the doctor and Silver come to terms, the doctor urges Jim to escape and retells Jim's actions and accomplishments.

I

. . . and after an obvious hesitation, he also hauled himself heavily into the shrouds, and, with the dirk in his teeth, began slowly and painfully to mount. It cost him no end of time and groans to haul his wounded leg behind him; and I had quietly finished my arrangements before he was much more than a third of the way up. Then, with a pistol in either hand, I addressed him.

"One more step, Mr. Hands," said I, "and I'll blow your brains out! Dead men don't bite, you know," I added, with a chuckle.

He stopped instantly. I could see by the working of his face that he was trying to think, and the process was so slow and laborious that, in my new-found security, I laughed aloud. At last, with a swallow or two, he spoke, his face still wearing the same expression of extreme perplexity. In order to speak he had to take the dagger from his mouth, but, in all else, he remained unmoved.

"Jim," says he, "I reckon we're fouled, you and me, and we'll have to sign articles. I'd have had you but for that there lurch: but I don't have no luck, not I; and I reckon I'll have to strike, which comes hard, you see, for a master mariner to a ship's younker like you, Jim."

I was drinking in his words, and smiling away, as conceited as a cock upon a wall, when, all in a breath, back went his right hand over his shoulder. Something sang like an arrow through the air: I felt a blow and then a sharp pang, and there I was pinned by the shoulder to the mast. In the horrid pain and surprise of the moment—I scarce can say it was by my own volition, and I am sure it was without a conscious aim—both my pistols went off, and both escaped out of my hands. They did not fall alone; with a choked cry, the coxswain loosed his grasp upon the shrouds, and plunged head first into the water.

II

The sea cook instantly removed his pipe.

"Now, look you here, Jim Hawkins," he said, in a steady whisper, that was no more than audible, "you're within half a plank of death, and, what's a long sight worse, of torture. They're going to throw me off. But, you mark, I stand by you through thick and thin. I didn't mean to; no, not till you spoke up. I was about desperate to lose that much blunt, and be hanged into the bargain. But I see you was the right sort. I says to myself: You stand by Hawkins, John, and Hawkins'll stand by you. You're his last card, and, by the living thunder, John, he's yours! Back to back, says I. You save your witness, and he'll save your neck!"

I began dimly to understand.

"You mean all's lost?" I asked.

"Ay, by gum, I do!" he answered. "Ship gone, neck gone—that's the size of it. Once I looked into that bay, Jim Hawkins, and seen no schooner—well, I'm tough, but I gave out. As for that lot and their council, mark me, they're outright fools and cowards. I'll save your life—if so be as I can—from them. But, see here, Jim—tit for tat—you save Long John from swinging."

I was bewildered; it seemed a thing so hopeless he was asking—he, the old buccaneer, the ringleader throughout.

"What I can do, that I'll do," I said.

"It's a bargain!" cried Long John. "You speak up plucky, and, by thunder! I've a chance."

He hobbled to the torch, where it stood propped among the firewood, and took a fresh light to his pipe.

"Understand me, Jim," he said, returning, "I've a head on my shoulders, I have. I'm on squire's side now. I know you've got that ship safe somewheres. How you done it, I don't know, but safe it is. I guess Hands and O'Brien turned soft. I never much believed in neither of *them*. Now you mark me, I ask no questions, nor I won't let others. I know when a game's up, I do; and I know a lad that's staunch. Ah, you that's young—you and me might have done a power of good together!"

He drew some cognac from the cask into a tin cannikin.

"Will you taste, messmate?" he asked; and when I had refused. "Well, I'll take a drain myself, Jim," said he. "I need a caulker, for there's trouble on hand. And, talking o' trouble, why did that doctor give me the chart, Jim?"

My face expressed a wonder so unaffected that he saw the needlessness of further questions.

"Ah, well, he did, though, " said he. "And there's something under that, no doubt—something, surely, under that, Jim—bad or good."

And he took another swallow of the brandy, shaking his great fair head like a man who looks forward to the worst.

III

"Jim," the doctor interrupted, and his voice was quite changed, "Jim, I can't have this. Whip over, and we'll run for it."

"Doctor," said I, "I passed my word."

"I know, I know," he cried. "We can't help that, Jim, now. I'll take it on my shoulders, holus bolus, blame and shame, my boy; but stay here, I cannot let you. Jump! One jump, and you're out, and we'll run for it like antelopes."

"No," I replied, "you know right well you wouldn't do the thing yourself; neither you, nor squire, nor captain; and no more will I. Silver trusted me; I passed my word, and back I go. But, doctor, you did not let me finish. If they come to torture me, I might let slip a word of where the ship is; for I got the ship, part by luck and part by risking, and she lies in North Inlet, on the southern beach, and just below high water. At half tide she must be high and dry."

"The ship!" exclaimed the doctor.

Rapidly I described to him my adventures, and he heard me out in silence.

"There is a kind of fate in this," he observed, when I had done. "Every step, it's you that saves our lives; and do you suppose by any chance that we are going to let you lose yours? That would be a poor return, my boy. You found out the plot; you found Ben Gunn—the best deed that ever you did, or will do, though you live to ninety. Oh, by Jupiter, and talking of Ben Gunn! why, this is the mischief in person. Silver!" he cried, "Silver!—I'll give you a piece of advice," he continued, as the cook drew near again; "don't you be in any great hurry after that treasure."

"Why, sir, I do my possible, which that ain't," said Silver. "I can only, asking your pardon, save my life and the boy's by seeking for that treasure; and you may lay to that."

"Well, Silver," replied the doctor, "if that is so, I'll go one step further: look out for squalls when you find it."

"Sir," said Silver, "as between man and man, that's too much and too little. What you're after, why you left the block-house, why you given me that there chart, I don't know, now, do I, and yet I done your bidding with my eyes shut and never a word of hope? But no, this here's too much. If you won't tell me what you mean plain out, just say so, and I'll leave the helm."

"No," said the doctor, musingly, "I've no right to say more; it's not my secret, you see, Silver, or, I give you my word, I'd tell it you. But I'll go as far with you as I dare go, and a step beyond; for I'll have my wig sorted by the captain or I'm mistaken!"

Questions

7. Treasure Island

1. Which of the following comes closest to the author's meaning when he titled his book *Treasure Island*?
   a. an imaginary island
   b. an island to be treasured in memory
   c. an island containing buried treasure
   d. an island with a vague promise of wealth

2. Which of the following phrases best expresses the meaning of " 'you're within *half a plank* of death' "?
   a. You are perilously close to death.
   b. Only the thickness of the planks of the ship's hull keeps you from drowning at this moment.
   c. We are shipwrecked, and clinging to half a plank.
   d. You will be forced to walk the plank at any moment.

3. Which of these character traits of Jim Hawkins is most forcefully brought out in the passage?
   a. anxiety
   b. pride
   c. honor
   d. courage

55

4. Which of the following best describes the tone of the passage?
   a. critical
   b. sympathetic
   c. satirical
   d. humorous

5. Which of the following best describes Long John Silver's point of view in the passage?
   a. fear of losing the treasure
   b. fear of his former shipmates
   c. fear of being hanged
   d. fear of Jim Hawkins

6. Which of the following best expresses the main theme of the passage?
   a. a philosophical discussion of the hazards and uncertainties of the adventurous life
   b. an attempt to justify Jim's murder of Mr. Hands
   c. an account of the fears, plans, and desperate acts of a group of men in terrible danger
   d. an explanation of the character and motives of Long John Silver

Pearl S. Buck

(1892-1973)

The Good Earth

Pearl S. Buck, best known as the author of *The Good Earth, Imperial Woman*, and other novels with a setting in China, wrote many books and articles of India, Japan, Korea, and America. She was born in Hillsboro, West Virginia, on June 26, 1892, and spent her early girlhood in China with her missionary parents. She came back to the United States at the time of the Boxer Rebellion, 1900, and was graduated from Randolph-Macon Woman's College, Lynchburg, Virginia, in 1914. Three years later she was married to John L. Buck, a Presbyterian missionary like herself, and returned to China.

After teaching in missionary schools, she embarked upon a literary career. Her first novel, set in China, was *East Wind, West Wind*, published in 1930, followed by *The Good Earth* (1931), *Sons* (1932), and *A House Divided* (1935), the last three comprising a trilogy called *The House of Earth*.

In 1933 she retired from missionary work, obtained a divorce, and in 1935 married Richard J. Walsh, president of the John Day Company, her New York publisher. In her new home in Bucks County, Pennsylvania, she completed *The Exile* (1936) and *Fighting Angel* (1936), which were biographies of her parents. Her other books include *The Patriot* (1939), *Other Gods* (1940), *Today and Forever* (1941), *Dragon Seed* (1942), *Pavilion of Women* (1946), *Kinfolk* (1949), and *One Bright Day* (1950). *Imperial Woman* (1956), a novel based upon the life of the Dowager Empress of China, was a widely read book and the basis for a successful drama. She was awarded the Nobel Prize for literature in 1938 and elected to the American Academy of Arts and Letters in 1951.

In the mid-1940s she determined to see if she could avoid being stereotyped as a writer solely of Chinese subjects; therefore she produced five novels in about five years under the pseudonym of John Sedges. Her sister, Cornelia Spencer, reports the results:

> Some people never suspected who the real author was. Those who did, realized that besides Pearl Buck's Chinese *style*, there was Pearl Buck's *touch*. They had been able to recognize her because of that touch and not because of any Chinese way of putting things. The humanness of her characters, not the style in which she had written them, had betrayed her.[1]

In fields other than literature, Pearl Buck also had a distinguished career—in support of aid for retarded children (her daughter was mentally retarded); in promoting adoption of orphans (especially those abandoned by parents of mixed races—she adopted five children into her own home and founded an adoptive agency, Welcome House); in lecturing and writing in support of better East-West understanding (she established the East-West association in New York City 1940-50); and in testifying against the internment of Japanese-Americans on the West Coast during World War II.

Three representative sections from *The Good Earth* are chosen for study. The first is from chapter 3, during the early struggles of the poor farmer, Wang Lung, and his wife, O-lan. The second is from chapter 30, when Wang Lung, now well-to-do, cautions his free-spending son. The third section, from chapter 34, reveals the aged farmer's regard for the good earth.

I

But there is not that about three rooms and two meals a day to keep busy a woman who has been a slave in a great house and who has worked from dawn until midnight. One day when Wang Lung was hard pressed with the swelling wheat and was cultivating it with his hoe, day after day, until his back throbbed with weariness, her shadow fell across the furrow over which he bent himself, and there she stood, with a hoe across her shoulder.

"There is nothing in the house until nightfall," she said briefly, and without speech she took the furrow to the left of him and fell into steady hoeing.

The sun beat down upon them, for it was early summer and her face was soon dripping with her sweat. Wang Lung had his coat off and his back bare, but she worked with her thin garment covering her shoulders and it grew wet and clung to her like skin. Moving together in a perfect rhythm, without a word, hour after hour, he fell into a union with her which took

---

[1] Cornelia Spencer, *Pearl S. Buck* (Chicago: Encyclopedia Britannica Press, 1964), p. 154.

the pain from his labor. He had no articulate thought of anything; there was only this perfect sympathy of movement, of turning this earth of theirs over and over to the sun, this earth which formed their home and fed their bodies and made their gods. The earth lay rich and dark, and fell apart lightly under the points of their hoes. Sometimes they turned up a bit of brick, a splinter of wood. It was nothing. Some time, in some age, bodies of men and women had been buried there, houses had stood there, had fallen, and gone back into the earth. So would also their house, some time, return into the earth, their bodies also. Each had his turn at this earth. They worked on, moving together—together—producing the fruit of this earth—speechless in their movement together.

When the sun had set he straightened his back slowly and looked at the woman. Her face was wet and streaked with the earth. She was as brown as the very soil itself. Her wet, dark garments clung to her square body. She smoothed a last furrow slowly. Then in her usual plain way she said, straight out, her voice flat and more than usually plain in the silent evening air,

"I am with child."

Wang Lung stood still. What was there to say to this thing then! She stooped to pick up a bit of broken brick and threw it out of the furrow. It was as though she had said, "I have brought you tea," or as though she had said, "We can eat." It seemed as ordinary as that to her! But to him—he could not say what it was to him. His heart swelled and stopped as though it met sudden confines. Well, it was their turn at this earth!

He took the hoe suddenly from her hand and he said, his voice thick in his throat, "Let be for now. It is a day's end. We will tell the old man."

They walked home, then, she half a dozen paces behind him as befitted a woman. The old man stood at the door, hungry for his evening's food, which, now that the woman was in the house, he would never prepare for himself. He was impatient and he called out,

"I am too old to wait for my food like this!"

But Wang Lung, passing him into the room, said,

"She is with child already."

He tried to say it easily as one might say, "I have planted the seeds in the western field today," but he could not. Although he spoke in a low voice it was to him as though he had shouted the words out louder than he would.

The old man blinked for a moment and then comprehended, and cackled with laughter.

"Heh-heh-heh—" he called out to his daughter-in-law as she came, "so the harvest is in sight!"

Her face he could not see in the dusk, but she answered evenly,

"I shall prepare food now."

"Yes—yes—food—" said the old man eagerly, following her into the kitchen like a child. Just as the thought of a grandson had made him forget his meal, so now the thought of food freshly before him made him forget the child.

But Wang Lung sat upon a bench by the table in the darkness and put his head upon his folded arms. Out of this body of his, out of his own loins, life!

When the hour for birth drew near he said to the woman,
"We must have someone to help at the time—some woman."

II

But he spoke that same evening to his eldest son, saying,
"Have done with all this painting and polishing. It is enough. We are, after all, country folk."
But the young man answered proudly,
"That we are not. Men in the town are beginning to call us the great family Wang. It is fitting that we live somewhat suitably to that name, and if my brother cannot see beyond the meaning of silver for its own sake, I and my wife, we will uphold the honor of the name."
Now Wang Lung had not known that men so called his house, for as he grew older he went seldom even to the tea shops and no more to the grain markets since there was his second son to do his business there for him, but it pleased him secretly and so he said,
"Well, even great families are from the land and rooted in the land."
But the young man answered smartly,
"Yes, but they do not stay there. They branch forth and bear flowers and fruits."
Wang Lung would not have his son answering him too easily and quickly like this, so he said,
"I have said what I have said. Have done with pouring out silver. And roots, if they are to bear fruit, must be kept well in the soil of the land."

III

"Child, what was it I wanted to say?"
And Pear Blossom answered gently,
"Where were you this day?"
"I was upon the land," Wang Lung replied, waiting, his eyes fixed on her face.
And she asked gently again,
"On what piece of land?"
Then suddenly the thing flew into his mind again and he cried, laughing out of his wet eyes,
"Well, and I do remember. My son, I have chosen my place in the earth, and it is below my father and his brother and above your mother and next to Ching, and I would see my coffin before I die."

Reading for Ideas

Then Wang Lung's eldest son cried out dutifully and properly,

"Do not say that word, my father, but I will do as you say."

Then his son brought a carven coffin hewn from a great log of fragrant wood which is used to bury the dead in and for nothing else because that wood is as lasting as iron, and more lasting than human bones, and Wang Lung was comforted.

And he had the coffin brought into his room and he looked at it every day.

Then all of a sudden he thought of something and he said,

"Well, and I would have it moved out to the earthen house and there I will live out my few days and there I will die."

And when they saw how he had set his heart they did what he wished and he went back to the house on his land, he and Pear Blossom and the fool, and what servants they needed; and Wang Lung took up his abode again on his land, and he left the house in the town to the family he had founded.

Spring passed and summer passed into harvest and in the hot autumn sun before winter comes Wang Lung sat where his father had sat against the wall. And he thought no more about anything now except his food and his drink and his land. But of his land he thought no more what harvest it would bring or what seed would be planted or of anything except of the land itself, and he stooped sometimes and gathered some of the earth up in his hand and he sat thus and held it in his hand, and it seemed full of life between his fingers. And he was content, holding it thus, and he thought of it fitfully and of his good coffin that was there; and the kind earth waited without haste until he came to it.

His sons were proper enough to him and they came to him every day or at most once in two days, and they sent him delicate food fit for his age, but he liked best to have one stir up meal in hot water and sup it as his father had done.

Questions

8. The Good Earth

1. In the sentence: "His heart swelled and stopped as though it met sudden confines," which of the following definitions best explains the use of the word *confines*?
    a. boundary
    b. enclosure
    c. restriction
    d. imprisonment

2. When Pearl Buck writes of Wang Lung: "he liked best to have one stir up meal in hot water and sup it as his father had done," which of the following best describes the author's use of the allusion *as his father had done*?
    a. This was a family custom.
    b. This shows the high regard he held for his father.
    c. The elderly Wang Lung chose to live simply.
    d. Wang Lung could not assimilate richer food.

3. Which of Wang Lung's traits of character is most clearly shown in the selections from *The Good Earth*?
    a. industry
    b. sympathy
    c. humility
    d. pride

4. Which of the following definitions best describes the tone of the passages selected from *The Good Earth*?
   a. satirical
   b. critical
   c. sympathetic
   d. serious and realistic

5. In which of the following statements is Pearl Buck's philosophy most clearly expressed?
   a. All men are brothers.
   b. Men grow strong by remaining close to the earth.
   c. Men grow strong through hard labor.
   d. Men grow strong through devotion to family.

6. Which of the following best describes the pattern of development of the novel, *The Good Earth*?
   a. a study of Chinese customs
   b. a narration of social life in China
   c. a realistic novel of a Chinese farm family
   d. a story of agricultural conditions in China

9

Sir Walter Scott

(1771-1832)

Ivanhoe

Born in Edinburgh of an old Border family, Walter Scott as a youth was a keen student of the region and an avid reader of romances and chronicles that were full of fighting, jousting, and crusades. He studied law and obtained two part-time positions (sheriff advocate and clerk of session), which left him ample opportunity for a literary career.

Scott's fame came to him first for his poems of the highlands: *The Lay of the Last Minstrel* (1805), *Marmion* (1808), and *Lady of the Lake* (1810). His novels, from *Guy Mannering* (1815) and the *Waverly Novels* (1816) to *Ivanhoe* (1820), *Kennilworth* (1821), and *The Tales of the Crusades* (1825), abound in battles, savagery, and bloodshed; in fact, bloodletting and torture furnish the thrills that made his prose so popular in his time and considerably so today. Scott's characters in historical settings are uncomplicated women and men either of deepest villainy or blameless courage. Typical are the three passages selected from *Ivanhoe*, Scott's most widely read romantic novel. The setting is England in 1194 at the time Richard I returned from the Third Crusade. This king is known as Richard the Lion-hearted, a name he earned by his courageous leadership in the Third Crusade. For that enterprise he had equipped 4,000 knights, 4,000 foot-soldiers, and a fleet of 100 transports; by 1191 he had conquered Cyprus, had inflicted a crushing defeat upon Saladin at Arsuf, and had led the Christian forces so close to Jerusalem that he exacted a favorable peace treaty. Under this treaty the Christians kept possession of the coast towns of Palestine and were granted free access to the Holy Sepulchre. Richard's amazing accomplishments, in the face of dissension among the Crusaders, were marred by his ruthless slaying of 2,700 Mohammedan prisoners. This was the brutal, lion-hearted man now using a vivid allusion to strike awe and fear into the heart of the Templar.

Scott was knighted in 1820. In 1826 he suffered three blows: he lost his wife, his health was greatly impaired, and he faced bankruptcy caused by unwise ventures in the publishing business and by personal extravagance. Although often in pain, he wrote voluminously the rest of his life and succeeded in liquidating the large part of his debts.

I

A short passage, and an ascent of seven steps, each of which was composed of a solid beam of oak, led him to the apartment of the Lady Rowena, the rude magnificence of which corresponded to the respect which was paid to her by the lord of the mansion. The walls were covered with embroidered hangings, on which different-coloured silks, interwoven with gold and silver threads, had been employed with all the art of which the age was capable, to represent the sports of hunting and hawking. The bed was adorned with the same rich tapestry, and surrounded with curtains dyed with purple. The seats had also their stained coverings, and one, which was higher than the rest, was accommodated with a footstool of ivory, curiously carved.

No fewer than four silver candelabra, holding great waxen torches, served to illuminate this apartment. Yet let not modern beauty envy the magnificence of a Saxon princess. The walls of the apartment were so ill finished and so full of crevices, that the rich hangings shook to the night blast, and, in spite of a sort of screen intended to protect them from the wind, the flame of the torches streamed sideways into the air, like the unfurled pennon of a chieftain. Magnificence there was, with some rude attempt at taste; but of comfort there was little, and, being unknown, it was unmissed.

II

Our scene now returns to the exterior of the Castle, or Preceptory, of Templestowe, about the hour when the bloody die was to be cast for the life or death of Rebecca. It was a scene of bustle and life, as if the whole vicinity had poured forth its inhabitants to a village wake, or rural feast. But the earnest desire to look on blood and death is not peculiar to those dark ages; though in the gladiatorial exercise of single combat and general tourney, they were habituated to the bloody spectacle of brave men falling by each other's hands. Even in our own days, when morals are better understood, an execution, a bruising match, a riot, or a meeting of radical reformers, collects, at considerable hazard to themselves, immense crowds of spectators, otherwise little interested, except to see how matters are to be conducted, or whether the heroes of the day are, in the heroic language of insurgent tailors, flints or dunghills.

The eyes, therefore, of a very considerable multitude, were bent on the gate of the Preceptory of Templestowe, with the purpose of witnessing the procession; while still greater numbers had already surrounded the tiltyard belonging to that establishment. This enclosure was formed on a piece of level ground adjoining to the Preceptory, which had been levelled with care, for the exercise of military and chivalrous sports. It occupied the brow of a soft and gentle eminence, was carefully palisaded around, and, as the Templars willingly invited spectators to be witnesses of their skill in feats of chivalry, was amply supplied with galleries and benches for their use.

III

"The stranger must first show," said Malvoisin, "That he is a good knight, and of honourable lineage. The Temple sendeth not forth her champions against nameless men."

"My name," said the Knight, raising his helmet, "is better known, my lineage more pure, Malvoisin, than thine own. I am Wilfred of Ivanhoe."

"I will not fight with thee at present," said the Templar, in a changed and hollow voice. "Get thy wounds healed, purvey thee a better horse, and it may be I will hold it worth my while to scourge out of thee this boyish spirit of bravade."

"Ha! proud Templar," said Ivanhoe, "hast thou forgotten that twice didst thou fall before this lance? Remember the lists at Acre—remember the Passage of Arms at Ashby—remember thy proud vaunt in the halls of Rotherwood, and the gage of your gold chain against my reliquary, that thou wouldst do battle with Wilfred of Ivanhoe, and recover the honour thou hadst lost! By that reliquary, and the holy relic it contains, I will proclaim thee, Templar, a coward in every court in Europe—in every Preceptory of thine Order—unless thou do battle without farther delay."

Bois-Guilbert turned his countenance irresolutely towards Rebecca, and then exclaimed, looking fiercely at Ivanhoe, "Dog of a Saxon! take thy lance, and prepare for the death thou has drawn upon thee!"

"Does the Grand Master allow me the combat?" said Ivanhoe.

"I may not deny that thou hast challenged," said the Grand Master, "provided the maiden accepts thee as her champion. Yet I would thou wert in better plight to do battle. An enemy of our Order hast thou ever been, yet would I have thee honourably met with."

"Thus—thus as I am, and not otherwise," said Ivanhoe; "it is the judgment of God—to his keeping I commend myself. —Rebecca," said he, riding up to the fatal chair, "dost thou accept of me for thy champion?"

"I do," she said—"I do," fluttered by an emotion which the fear of death had been unable to produce, "I do accept thee as the champion whom

Heaven hath sent me. Yet, no—no—thy wounds are uncured. — Meet not that proud man—why shouldst thou perish also?"

But Ivanhoe was already at his post, and had closed his visor, and assumed his lance. Bois-Guilbert did the same; and his esquire remarked, as he clasped his visor, that his face, which had, notwithstanding the variety of emotions by which he had been agitated, continued during the whole morning of an ashy paleness, was now become suddenly very much flushed.

The herald, then, seeing each champion in his place, uplifted his voice, repeating thrice—*Faites vos devoirs, preux chevaliers!* After the third cry, he withdrew to one side of the lists, and again proclaimed, that none, on peril of instant death, should dare, by word, cry, or action, to interfere with, or disturb this fair field of combat. The Grand Master, who held in his hand the gage of battle, Rebecca's glove, now threw it into the lists, and pronounced the fatal signal words, *Laissez aller.*

The trumpets sounded, and the knights charged each other in full career. The wearied horse of Ivanhoe, and its no less exhausted rider, went down, as all had expected, before the well-aimed lance and vigorous steed of the Templar. This issue of the combat all had foreseen; but although the spear of Ivanhoe did but, in comparison, touch the shield of Bois-Guilbert, that champion, to the astonishment of all who beheld it, reeled in his saddle, lost his stirrups, and fell in the lists.

Ivanhoe, extricating himself from his fallen horse, was soon on foot, hastening to mend his fortune with his sword; but his antagonist arose not. Wilfred, placing his foot on his breast, and the sword's point to his throat, commanded him to yield him, or die on the spot. Bois-Guilbert returned no answer.

"Slay him not, Sir Knight," cried the Grand Master, "unshriven and unabsolved—kill not body and soul! We allow him vanquished."

He descended into the lists, and commanded them to unhelm the conquered champion. His eyes were closed—the dark red flush was still on his brow. As they looked on him in astonishment, the eyes opened—but they were fixed and glazed. The flush passed from his brow and gave way to the pallid hue of death. Unscathed by the lance of his enemy, he had died a victim to the violence of his own contending passions.

"This is indeed the judgment of God," said the Grand Master, looking upwards— *"Fiat voluntas tua!"*

When the first moments of surprise were over, Wilfred of Ivanhoe demanded of the Great Master, as judge of the field, if he had manfully and rightfully done his duty in the combat?

"Manfully and rightfully hath it been done," said the Grand Master; "I pronounce the main free and guiltless. — The arms and the body of the deceased knight are at the will of the victor."

"I will not despoil him of his weapons," said the Knight of Ivanhoe, "nor condemn his corpse to shame—he hath fought for Christendom—God's arm, no human hand, hath this day struck him down. But let his obsequies be private, as becomes those of a man who died in an unjust quarrel. —And for the maiden—"

He was interrupted by a clattering of horses' feet, advancing in such numbers, and so rapidly, as to shake the ground before them; and the Black Knight galloped into the lists. He was followed by a numerous band of men-at-arms, and several knights in complete armour.

"I am too late," he said, looking around him. "I had doomed Bois-Guilbert for mine own property. —Ivanhoe, was this well to take on thee such a venture, and thou scarce able to keep thy saddle?"

"Heaven, my Liege," answered Ivanhoe, "hath taken this proud man for its victim. He was not to be honoured in dying as your will had designed."

"Peace be with him," said Richard, looking steadfastly on the corpse, "if it may be so—he was a gallant knight, and has died in his steel harness full knightly. But we must waste no time—Bohun, do thine office!"

A Knight stepped forward from the King's attendants, and, laying his hand on the shoulder of Albert de Malvoisin, said, "I arrest thee of High Treason."

The Grand Master had hitherto stood astonished at the appearance of so many warriors. — He now spoke.

"Who dares to arrest a Knight of the Temple of Zion, within the girth of his own Preceptory, and in the presence of the Grand Master? and by whose authority is this bold outrage offered?"

"I make the arrest," replied the Knight— "I, Henry Bohun, Earl of Essex, Lord High Constable of England."

"And he arrests Malvoisin," said the King, raising his visor, "by the order of Richard Plantagenet, here present. —Conrade Mont-Fitchet, it is well for thee thou art born no subject of mine. —But for thee, Malvoisin, thou diest with thy brother Philip, ere the world be a week older."

"I will resist thy doom," said the Grand Master.

"Proud Templar," said the King, "thou canst not—look up, and behold the Royal Standard of England floats over thy towers instead of thy Temple banners! —Be wise, Beaumanoir, and make no bootless opposition. Thy hand is in the lion's mouth."

"I will appeal to Rome against thee," said the Grand Master, "for usurpation on the immunities and privileges of our Order."

Questions

9. Ivanhoe

1. Which of the following is the best definition of the word *allow* as used in the sentence: " 'We allow him vanquished' "?
   a. acknowledge
   b. permit
   c. assign
   d. grant

2. What did King Richard have in mind in alluding to the *lion's mouth* when he told Beaumanoir, " 'Thy hand is in the lion's mouth' "?
   a. King Richard meant that he had Beaumanoir in his power.
   b. King Richard pointed to the decline of the Templar's strength.
   c. He warned the Templar against a possible treasonable act.
   d. He advised the Templar to be wise.

3. Which of the following best describes the author's depiction of Ivanhoe's character?
   a. braggadocio
   b. prowess in battle
   c. gallantry
   d. determination

4. Which of the following definitions best describes the tone of the last two passages selected from Scott's *Ivanhoe*?
   a. suspenseful and thrilling
   b. realistic and lively
   c. impersonal
   d. romantic

5. Which of the following sentences best expresses the author's philosophic attitude in this selection?
   a. The best measure of a man is how he conducts himself in a crisis.
   b. Battle brings out the best in men.
   c. Knight errantry was a worthy calling in spite of its violence.
   d. Witch-burning was a hideous crime especially when justified as a Christian act.

6. Which of the following expressions best describes the pattern of development in the selected passages?
   a. a satire directed against chivalry
   b. a study of knightly bravery
   c. a series of twelfth-century episodes
   d. a fictional romance in a true historic setting

10

Sinclair Lewis

(1887-1951)

Arrowsmith

At the height of his creative power in the early 1920s, Sinclair Lewis sought a subject suitable for the idealism that had been overshadowed and suppressed by his heavy satire in *Main Street* (1920) and *Babbitt* (1922). He chose medicine partly because of his respect for his father and brother, who were doctors, and partly as a result of meeting Paul de Kruif, a prominent bacteriologist. The novel that grew out of these influences was *Arrowsmith* (1925).

Here he presents a hero in Dr. Martin Arrowsmith who discards the advantages of social position to give himself completely to lifesaving research in bacteriology. The author attacks the shallowness of the well-to-do and the commercial attitude of medical institutions as he presents in contrast the unselfish spirit of Arrowsmith—a man devoted to his profession.

In 1926 Lewis refused to accept a Pulitzer Prize for *Arrowsmith* because the committee had overlooked his earlier novels. However, he did go to Sweden in 1930 to receive the Nobel Award for Literature, an award based upon his total work. He was the first American to be so honored.

Lewis was a most cantankerous individual, quarreling with his publisher and other writers, divorcing each of his two wives, and paying scant attention to his two sons. He was annoyed by the meteoric rise to fame of his second wife, Dorothy Thompson, an outspoken journalist who was expelled from Germany by Hitler in 1934 and whose newspaper column and radio broadcasts helped prepare America to support Britain in World War II. Lewis left Miss Thompson for a short but indifferent career in the theater as playwright and actor—and he died a lonely man in Rome at age sixty-four.

Now, here is the setting for the novel: Having been forced to resign his position as director of Public Health in a small midwestern town because of political chicanery, Martin Arrowsmith welcomes the opportunity (made possible by Angus Duer, a friend and an ambitious classmate at medical school) to join the fashionable private Rouncefield Clinic as a pathologist.

In the first section, Arrowsmith and his wife, Leora (an intelligent, small-town girl, raised on the wheatfields of the Middle West), are in a taxi on their way home after an evening with the sophisticated social set of the Rouncefield Clinic's medical staff. Arrowsmith had just finished scolding Leora for appearing so uninformed by not taking part in the evening's conversations.

In section 2, the work at the Rouncefield Clinic, with its emphasis on commercialism and profit making, is becoming increasingly irritating to Arrowsmith. So, the letter from Dr. Max Gottlieb, his highly-respected former professor at medical school, is received with great joy and pride, both because of the opportunity to work under Gottlieb, and to be affiliated with an institute known for its dedication to fundamental research.

In section 3, the bubonic plague had broken out on an island in the West Indies. An urgent appeal for help was sent to the McGurk Institute because it was well known that Dr. Arrowsmith had done much research on an antitoxin named bacteriophage which might eradicate plague. (Dr. Arrowsmith shortened the name to *phage*.) Before leaving, Dr. Gottlieb made Arrowsmith promise to carry out an experiment of using the phage with only half his patients and keeping the others as an experimental control group to make an absolute determination of its value. Here, in selection quoted, Martin Arrowsmith is already at work on the plague-ridden island.

In section 4, with the plague sharply abating, Martin Arrowsmith is preparing to leave the island to return to his work. His wife, Leora, had come to the island with him, but now is dead—a victim of the plague.

I

She sat straight now, and when she spoke she had lost the casual independence with which she usually regarded life:

"Dear, I'm awfully sorry. I went out this afternoon, I went out and had a facial massage, so as to look nice for you, and then I knew you like conversation, so I got my little book about modern painting that I bought and I studied it terribly hard, but to-night, I just couldn't seem to get the conversation around to modern painting—"

She was sobbing, with her head on his shoulder, "Oh, you poor, scared, bullied kid, trying to be grown-up with these dollar-chasers!"

II

After the first daze of white tile and bustling cleverness at the Rouncefield Clinic, Martin had the desire to tie up a few loose knots of his streptolysin research.

When Angus Duer discovered it he hinted, "Look here, Martin, I'm glad you're keeping on with your science, but if I were you I wouldn't, I think, waste too much energy on mere curiosity. Dr. Rouncefield was speaking about it the other day. We'd be glad to have you do all the research you want, only we'd like it if you went at something practical. Take for instance: if you could make a tabulation of the blood-counts in a couple of hundred cases of appendicitis and publish it, that'd get somewhere, and you could sort of bring in a mention of the clinic, and we'd all receive a little credit—and incidentally maybe we could raise you to three thousand a year then."

This generosity had the effect of extinguishing Martin's desire to do any research whatever.

"Angus is right. What he means is: as a scientist I'm finished. I am. I'll never try to do anything original again."

It was at this time, when Martin had been with the clinic for a year, that his streptolysin paper was published in the *Journal of Infectious Diseases*. He gave reprints to Rouncefield and to Angus. They said extremely nice things which showed that they had not read the paper, and again they suggested his tabulating blood-counts.

He also sent a reprint to Max Gottlieb, at the McGurk Institute of Biology.

Gottlieb wrote him, in that dead-black spider-web script:

Dear Martin:
    I have read your paper with great pleasure. The curves of the relation of hemolysin production to age of culture are illuminating. I have spoken about you to Tubbs. When are you coming to us—to me? Your laboratory and diener are waiting for you here. The last thing I want to be is a mystic, but I feel when I see your fine engraved letterhead of a clinic and a Rouncefield that you should be tired of trying to be a good citizen and ready to come back to work. We shall be glad, & Dr. Tubbs, if you can come.
                                  Truly yours,
                                      M. Gottlieb.

"I'm simply going to adore New York," said Leora.

III

The plague had only begun to invade St. Swithin's but it was unquestionably coming, and Martin, with his power as official medical officer of the parish, was able to make plans. He divided his population into two equal parts. One of them, driven in by Twyford, was injected with plague phage, the other half was left without.

He began to succeed. He saw far-off India, with its annual four hundred thousand deaths from plague, saved by his efforts. He heard Max Gottlieb saying, "Martin, you haf done your experiment. I am very glat!"

The pest attacked the unphaged half of the parish much more heavily than those who had been treated. There did appear a case or two among those who had the phage, but among the others there were ten, then twenty, then thirty daily victims. These unfortunate cases he treated, giving the phage to alternate patients, in the somewhat barren almshouse of the parish, a whitewashed cabin the meaner against its vaulting background of banyans and breadfruit trees.

IV

When Martin was completing his notes he had a letter from the McGurk Institute, signed by Rippleton Holabird.

Holabird wrote that Gottlieb was "feeling seedy," that he had resigned the Directorship, suspended his own experimentation, and was now at home, resting. Holabird himself had been appointed Acting Director of the Institute, and as such he chanted:

> The reports of your work in the letters from Mr. McGurk's agents which the quarantine authorities have permitted to get through to us apprize us far more than does your own modest report what a really sensational success you have had. You have done what few other men living could do, both established the value of bacteriophage in plague by tests on a large scale, and saved most of the unfortunate population. The Board of Trustees and I are properly appreciative of the glory which you have added, and still more will add when your report is published, to the name of McGurk Institute, and we are thinking, now that we may for some months be unable to have your titular chief, Dr. Gottlieb, working with us, of establishing a separate Department, with you as its head.

"Established the value—rats! I about half made the tests," sighed Martin, and "Department! I've given too many orders here. Sick of authority. I want to get back to my lab and start all over again."

Questions

10. Arrowsmith

1. Which of the following purposes did Sinclair Lewis probably have in mind when choosing the name Arrowsmith for the central character of this novel?
   a. He wanted to use a distinctive name that readers would remember.
   b. He wanted a dignified name for a member of the medical profession.
   c. He chose a name that could have an American Indian connotation.
   d. He selected a name that suggests a man pointing to a definite goal in life.

2. Which of the following sentences best expresses the descriptive words italicized in: "Gottlieb wrote to him, in that dead-black *spider-web* script"?
   a. Gottlieb's script wove a web to entrap Arrowsmith.
   b. Gottlieb's script was fine, old-fashioned, and perhaps monotonous.
   c. Gottlieb's script showed his patience.
   d. Gottlieb's script wandered all over the page.

3. Which of Martin Arrowsmith's traits of character is most forcefully brought out in the selected passages?
   a. sympathy
   b. indecisiveness
   c. disgust
   d. perseverance

4. Which of the following definitions best describes the tone of the passages selected from *Arrowsmith*?
   a. critical
   b. satirical
   c. optimistic
   d. insincere

5. Which of the following statements best expresses the author's philosophic attitude?
   a. Research is the answer to many of mankind's ills.
   b. Lewis is urging freedom from hypocrisy.
   c. Lewis is satirizing the attitude of medical institutions.
   d. A man should strive for a high personal goal.

6. Which of the following phrases best describes the pattern of development?
   a. a story of medical research
   b. a fictional biography
   c. a criticism of well-to-do society
   d. a criticism of medical institutions

11

Eudora Welty
(1909-   )

A Worn Path

Of special interest about Eudora Welty is that she had a fling at writing advertising copy before becoming a writer of short stories and novels. Born in Jackson, Mississippi, she attended Mississippi State College for Women 1925-27, received her B.A. degree at the University of Wisconsin in 1929, and studied advertising at Columbia University 1930-31. After a short career in advertising, she returned to Jackson, Mississippi, where she, like William Faulkner, achieved fame as a regional writer. Her first publication, *A Curtain of Green*, in 1941, was a collection of stories, followed by *The Robber Bridegroom*, a novella, in 1942. *Delta Wedding* (1946) was her first full-length novel. *The Golden Apples* appeared in 1949 and *The Bride of Innisfallen* in 1955.

For *The Ponder Heart* (1954), a short novel, she was awarded the Howells Medal the following year. This is an honor bestowed every five years by the American Academy of Arts and Letters for the most distinguished work of American fiction. Miss Welty is an honorary consultant in American Letters for the Library of Congress.

The selections for study are taken from "A Worn Path," a short story typical of Miss Welty's concentration upon her home state and its people.

It was December—a bright frozen day in the early morning. Far out in the country there was an old Negro woman with her head tied in a red rag, coming along a path through the pinewoods. Her name was Phoenix Jackson.

She was very old and small and she walked slowly in the dark pine shadows, moving a little from side to side in her steps, with the balanced heaviness and lightness of a pendulum in a grandfather clock. She carried a thin, small cane made from an umbrella, and with this she kept tapping the frozen earth in front of her. This made a grave and persistent noise in the still air, that seemed meditative like the chirping of a solitary little bird.

She wore a dark striped dress reaching down to her shoe tops, and an equally long apron of bleached sugar sacks, with a full pocket: all neat and tidy, but every time she took a step she might have fallen over her shoelaces, which dragged from her unlaced shoes. She looked straight ahead. Her eyes were blue with age. Her skin had a pattern all its own of numberless branching wrinkles and as though a whole little tree stood in the middle of her forehead, but a golden color ran underneath, and the two knobs of her cheeks were illumined by a yellow burning under the dark. Under the red rag her hair came down on her neck in the frailest of ringlets, still black, and with an odor like copper.

Now and then there was a quivering in the thicket. Old Phoenix said, "Out of my way, all you foxes, owls, beetles, jack rabbits, coons and wild animals! . . . Keep out from under these feet, little bob-whites . . . Keep the big wild hogs out of my path. Don't let none of those come running my direction. I got a long way."

. . .

She paused quietly on the sidewalk where people were passing by. A lady came along in the crowd, carrying an armful of red- green- and silver-wrapped presents; she gave off perfume like the red roses in hot summer, and Phoenix stopped her.

"Please, missy, will you lace up my shoe?" She held up her foot.

"What do you want, Grandma?"

"See my shoe," said Phoenix. "Do all right for out in the country, but wouldn't look right to go in a big building."

"Stand still then, Grandma," said the lady. She put her packages down on the sidewalk beside her and laced and tied both shoes tightly. "Can't lace 'em with a cane," said Phoenix. "Thank you, missy. I doesn't mind asking a nice lady to tie up my shoe, when I gets out on the street."

Moving slowly and from side to side, she went into the big building, and into a tower of steps where she walked up and around and around until her feet knew to stop.

She entered a door, and there she saw nailed up on the wall the document that had been stamped with a gold seal and framed in the gold frame, which matched the dream that was hung up in her head.

"Here I be," she said. There was a fixed and ceremonial stiffness over her body.

"A charity case, I suppose," said an attendant who sat at the desk before her.

But Phoenix only looked above her head. There was sweat on her face, the wrinkles in her skin shone like a bright net.

"Speak up, Grandma," the woman said. "What's your name? We must have your history, you know. Have you been here before? What seems to be the trouble with you?"

Old Phoenix only gave a twitch to her face as if a fly were bothering her.

"Are you deaf?" cried the attendant.

But then the nurse came in.

"Oh, that's just old Aunt Phoenix," she said. "She doesn't come for herself—she has a little grandson. She makes these trips just as regular as clockwork. She lives away back off the Old Natchez Trace." She bent down. "Well, Aunt Phoenix, why don't you just take a seat? We won't keep you standing after your long trip." She pointed.

The old woman sat down, bolt upright in the chair.

"Now, how is the boy?" asked the nurse.

Old Phoenix did not speak.

"I said, how is the boy?"

But Phoenix only waited and stared straight ahead, her face very solemn and withdrawn into rigidity.

"Is his throat any better?" asked the nurse. "Aunt Phoenix, don't you hear me? Is your grandson's throat any better since the last time you came for the medicine?"

With her hands on her knees, the old woman waited, silent, erect and motionless, just as if she were in armor.

"You mustn't take up our time this way, Aunt Phoenix," the nurse said. "Tell us quickly about your grandson, and get it over. He isn't dead, is he?"

At last there came a flicker and then a flame of comprehension across her face, and she spoke.

"My grandson. It was my memory had left me. There I sat and forgot why I made my long trip."

"Forgot?" The nurse frowned. "After you came so far?"

Then Phoenix was like an old woman begging a dignified forgiveness for waking up frightened in the night. "I never did go to school, I was too old at the Surrender," she said in a soft voice. "I'm an old woman without an education. It was my memory fail me. My little grandson, he is just the same, and I forgot it in the coming."

"Throat never heals, does it?" said the nurse, speaking in a loud, sure voice to old Phoenix. By now she had a card with something written on it, a little list. "Yes. Swallowed lye. When was it?—January—two-three years ago—"

Phoenix spoke unasked now. "No, missy, he not dead, he just the same. Every little while his throat begin to close up again, and he not able to swallow. He not get his breath. He not able to help himself. So the time come around, and I go on another trip for the soothing medicine."

"All right. The doctor said as long as you came to get it, you could have it," said the nurse. "But it's an obstinate case."

"My little grandson, he sit up there in the house all wrapped up, waiting by himself," Phoenix went on. "We is the only two left in the world. He suffer and it don't seem to put him back at all. He got a sweet look. He going to last. He wear a little patch quilt and peep out holding his mouth open like a little bird. I remembers so plain now. I not going to forget him again, no, the whole enduring time. I could tell him from all the others in creation."

"All right." The nurse was trying to hush her now. She brought her a bottle of medicine. "Charity," she said, making a check mark in a book.

Old Phoenix held the bottle close to her eyes, and then carefully put it into her pocket.

"I thank you," she said.

"It's Christmas time, Grandma," said the attendant. "Could I give you a few pennies out of my purse?"

"Five pennies is a nickel," said Phoenix stiffly.

"Here's a nickel," said the attendant.

Phoenix rose carefully and held out her hand. She received the nickel and then fished the other nickel out of her pocket and laid it beside the new one. She stared at her palm closely, with her head on one side.

Then she gave a tap with her cane on the floor.

"This is what come to me to do," she said. "I going to the store and buy my child a little windmill they sells, made out of paper. He going to find it hard to believe there such a thing in the world. I'll march myself back where he waiting, holding it straight up in this hand."

She lifted her free hand, gave a little nod, turned around, and walked out of the doctor's office. Then her slow step began on the stairs going down.

Reading for Ideas

Questions

11. A Worn Path

1. Which of the following statements best explains the significance of the name *Phoenix*, the central character in "A Worn Path"?

   a. It emphasized Phoenix Jackson's advanced age.
   b. It is typical of many southerners' desire to have a dressy or romantic name.
   c. It helped qualify Phoenix Jackson for our highest respect.
   d. It emphasized an almost indestructible source of strength in a very old body.

2. What does the author accomplish by comparing the grave and persistent noise of the tapping cane to "the chirping of a solitary little bird"?

   a. emphasizes that the time of the story is winter
   b. points to the woman's need to use a cane
   c. says that Aunt Phoenix is as little and as solitary as a bird
   d. carries out an analogy with the legendary Phoenix

3. Which of Phoenix Jackson's character traits is most forcefully brought out in the passages from "A Worn Path"?

   a. perseverance
   b. humility
   c. love
   d. kindness

4. Which of the following definitions best describes the tone of the passages selected from "A Worn Path"?
   a. charitable
   b. sympathetic
   c. critical
   d. ironic

5. Which of the following expressions best reveals the author's philosophic attitude?
   a. Every person has a basic dignity.
   b. Human values are more important than education.
   c. Human values are more important than race.
   d. Love transcends death.

6. Which of the following phrases best describes the pattern of development of the short story, "A Worn Path"?
   a. a realistic tale of southern life
   b. an explanation of a woman's regeneration
   c. an example of symbolism
   d. a story of love

12

Charles Dickens
(1812-1870)

A Tale of Two Cities

A Tale of Two Cities, London and Paris, is a historical romance of the time of the French Revolution. It differs from most of Dickens' other works in that it has relatively few characters, little humorous relief, and little social criticism except for relatively brief references to the excesses of the revolutionists and of the earlier French nobility. It concerns the lives of two men, Sidney Carton (an Englishman) and Charles Darnay (or Evrémonde, a Frenchman), who look alike and who are suitors of Lucie Manette. Darnay marries Lucie but is caught up in the Reign of Terror in Paris and condemned to death for the crimes of his aristocratic ancestors. Carton, still devoted to Lucie, takes Darnay's place at the guillotine and becomes one of literature's outstanding examples of a man giving his life for love of another (in this case for love of Lucie).

Besides the heroic figure of Sidney Carton, Dickens presents the revengeful revolutionist Madame Defarge whose intense hatred of the aristocrats inflames the blood-thirsty tribunals. Section 1 gives (a) a glimpse of Carton posing as Darnay (Evrémonde) on the way to the gallows, and (b) an incident in the escape to safety of Lucie with her father, daughter, and her husband, Darnay. Section 2 describes the conference of Madame Defarge with the revolutionary jurors, The Vengeance and Jacques Three, in which they plan how to give incriminating evidence against Darnay. Section 3 covers the actions and thoughts of Carton as he approaches the executioner.

Reprinted from *A Tale of Two Cities*, by Charles Dickens. Used by permission of the publisher, Allyn & Bacon, Inc.

I

The door closed, and Carton was left alone. Straining his powers of listening to the utmost, he listened for any sound that might denote suspicion or alarm. There was none. Keys turned, doors clashed, footsteps passed along distant passages; no cry was raised, or hurry made, that seemed unusual. Breathing more freely in a little while, he sat down at the table, and listened again until the clock struck Two.

Sounds that he was not afraid of, for he divined their meaning, then began to be audible. Several doors were opened in succession, and finally his own. A gaoler, with a list in his hand, looked in, merely saying, "Follow me, Evrémonde!" and he followed into a large dark room, at a distance. It was a dark winter day, and what with the shadows within, and what with the shadows without, he could but dimly discern the others who were brought there to have their arms bound. Some were standing; some seated. Some were lamenting, and in restless motion; but these were few. The great majority were silent and still, looking fixedly at the ground.

As he stood by the wall in a dim corner, while some of the fifty-two were brought in after him, one man stopped in passing, to embrace him, as having a knowledge of him. It thrilled him with a great dread of discovery; but the man went on. A very few moments after that, a young woman, with a slight girlish form, a sweet spare face in which there was no vestige of colour, and large widely opened patient eyes, rose from the seat where he had observed her sitting, and came to speak to him.

"Citizen Evrémonde," she said, touching him with her cold hand. "I am a poor little seamstress, who was with you in La Force."

He murmured for answer: "True. I forget what you were accused of?"

"Plots. Though the just Heaven knows I am innocent of any. Is it likely? Who would think of plotting with a poor little weak creature like me?"

The forlorn smile with which she said it, so touched him, that tears started from his eyes.

"I am not afraid to die, Citizen Evrémonde, but I have done nothing. I am not unwilling to die, if the Republic, which is to do so much good to us poor, will profit by my death; but I do not know how that can be, Citizen Evrémonde. Such a poor weak little creature!"

As the last thing on earth that his heart was to warm and soften to, it warmed and softened to this pitiable girl.

"I heard you were released, Citizen Evrémonde. I hoped it was true?"

"It was. But, I was again taken and condemned."

"If I may ride with you, Citizen Evrémonde, will you let me hold your hand? I am not afraid, but am little and weak, and it will give me more courage."

As the patient eyes were lifted to his face, he saw a sudden doubt in them, and then astonishment. He pressed the work-worn, hunger-worn young fingers and touched his lips.

"Are you dying for him?" she whispered.

"And his wife and child. Hush! Yes."

"O you will let me hold your brave hand, stranger?"

"Hush! Yes, my poor sister; to the last."

The same shadows that are falling on the prison, are falling, in that same hour of the early afternoon, on the Barrier with the crowd about it, when a coach going out of Paris drives up to be examined.

"Who goes here? Whom have we within? Papers!"

The papers are handed out, and read.

"Alexandre Manette. Physician. French. Which is he?"

This is he; this helpless, inarticulately murmuring, wandering old man pointed out.

"Apparently the Citizen-Doctor is not in his right mind? The Revolution fever will have been too much for him?"

Greatly too much for him.

"Hah! Many suffer with it. Lucie. His daughter. French. Which is she?"

This is she.

"Apparently it must be. Lucie, the wife of Evrémonde; is it not?"

It is.

"Hah! Evrémonde has an assignation elsewhere. Lucie, her child. English. This is she?"

She and no other.

"Kiss me, child of Evrémonde. Now thou hast kissed a good Republican; something new in thy family; remember it! Sidney Carton. Advocate. English. Which is he?"

He lies here, in this corner of the carriage. He, too, is pointed out.

"Apparently the English advocate is in a swoon?"

It is hoped he will recover in the fresher air. It is represented that he is not in strong health, and has separated sadly from a friend who is under the displeasure of the Republic.

"Is that all? It is not a great deal, that! Many are under the displeasure of the Republic, and must look out at the little window. Jarvis Lorry. Banker. English. Which is he?"

"I am he. Necessarily, being the last."

It is Jarvis Lorry who has replied to all the previous questions. It is Jarvis Lorry who has alighted and stands with his hand on the coach door, replying to a group of officials. They leisurely walked round the carriage and leisurely mount the box, to look at what little luggage it carries on the roof; the country people hanging about, press nearer to the coach doors and greedily stare in; a little child, carried by its mother, has its short arm held out for it, that it may touch the wife of an aristocrat who has gone to the Guillotine.

"Behold your papers, Jarvis Lorry, countersigned."

"One can depart, citizen?"

"One can depart. Forward, my postilions? A good journey!"

"I salute you, citizens. —And the first danger passed!"

These are again the words of Jarvis Lorry, as he clasps his hands, and looks upward.

II

In that same same juncture of time when the Fifty-Two awaited their fate, Madame Defarge held darkly ominous council with The Vengeance and Jacques Three of the Revolutionary Jury. Not in the wineshop did Madame Defarge confer with these ministers, but in the shed of the wood-sawyer, erst a mender of roads. The sawyer himself did not participate in the conference, but abided at a little distance, like an outer satellite who was not to speak until required, or to offer an opinion until invited.

"But our Defarge," said Jacques Three, "is undoubtedly a good Republican? Eh?"

"There is no better," the voluble Vengeance protested in her shrill notes, "in France."

"Peace, little Vengeance," said Madame Defarge, laying her hand with a slight frown on her lieutenant's lips, "hear me speak. My husband, fellow-citizen, is a good Republican and a bold man; he has deserved well of the Republic, and possesses its confidence. But my husband has his weaknesses, and he is so weak as to relent towards this Doctor."

"It is a great pity," croaked Jacques Three, dubiously shaking his head, with his cruel fingers at his hungry mouth; "it is not quite like a good citizen; it is a thing to regret."

"See you," said madame, "I care nothing for this Doctor, I. He may wear his head or lose it, for any interest I have in him; it is all one to me. But, the Evrémonde people are to be exterminated, and the wife and child must follow the husband and father."

"She has a fine head for it," croaked Jacques Three. "I have seen blue eyes and golden hair there, and they looked charming when Samson held them up." Ogre that he was, he spoke like an epicure.

Madame Defarge cast down her eyes, and reflected a little.

"The child also," observed Jacques Three, with a meditative enjoyment of his words, "has golden hair and blue eyes. And we seldom have a child there. It is a pretty sight!"

"In a word," said Madame Defarge, coming out of her short abstraction, "I cannot trust my husband in this matter. Not only do I feel, since last night, that I dare not confide to him the details of my projects; but I also feel that if I delay, there is danger of his giving warning, and then they might escape."

"That must never be," croaked Jacques Three; "no one must escape. We have not half enough as it is. We ought to have six score a day."

"In a word," Madame Defarge went on, "my husband has not my reason for pursuing this family to annihilation, and I have not his reason for regarding this Doctor with any sensibility. I must act for myself, therefore. Come hither, little citizen."

The wood-sawyer, who held her in the respect and himself in the submission, of mortal fear, advanced with his hand to his red cap.

"Touching those signals, little citizen," said Madame Defarge, sternly, "that she made to the prisoners; you are ready to bear witness to them this very day?"

"Ay, ay, why not!" cried the sawyer. "Every day, in all weathers, from two to four, always signalling, sometimes with the little one, sometimes without. I know what I know. I have seen with my eyes."

He made all manner of gestures while he spoke, as if in incidental imitation of some few of the great diversity of signals that he had never seen.

"Clearly plots," said Jacques Three. "Transparently!"

"There is no doubt of the Jury?" inquired Madame Defarge, letting her eyes turn to him with a gloomy smile.

"Rely upon the patriotic Jury, dear citizeness. I answer for my fellow-Jurymen."

"Now, let me see," said Madame Defarge, pondering again. "Yet once more! Can I spare this Doctor to my husband? I have no feeling either way. Can I spare him?"

"He would count as one head," observed Jacques Three, in a low voice. "We really have not heads enough; it would be a pity, I think."

"He was signalling with her when I saw her," argued Madame Defarge; "I cannot speak of one without the other; and I must not be silent, and trust the case wholly to him, this little citizen here. For I am not a bad witness."

The Vengeance and Jacques Three vied with each other in their fervent protestations that she was the most admirable and marvellous of witnesses. The little citizen, not to be outdone, declared her to be a celestial witness.

"He must take his chance," said Madame Defarge. "No, I cannot spare him! You are engaged at three o'clock; you are going to see the batch of to-day executed. —You?"

The question was addressed to the wood-sawyer, who hurriedly replied in the affirmative: seizing the occasion to add that he was the most ardent of Republicans, and that he would be in effect the most desolate of Republicans, if anything prevented him from enjoying the pleasure of smoking his afternoon pipe in the contemplation of the droll national barber. He was so very demonstrative herein, that he might have been suspected (perhaps was, by the dark eyes that looked contemptuously at him out of Madame Defarge's head) of having his small individual fears for his own personal safety, every hour of the day.

"I," said madame, "am equally engaged at the same place. After it is over—say at eight tonight—come you to me, in Saint Antoine, and we will give information against these people at my Section."

The wood-sawyer said he would be proud and flattered to attend the citizeness. The citizeness looking at him, he became embarrassed, evaded her glance as a small dog would have done.

III

She goes next before him—is gone; the knitting-women count Twenty-Two.

"I am the Resurrection and the Life, saith the Lord: he that believeth in me, though he were dead yet shall he live: and whosoever liveth and believeth in me shall never die!"

The murmuring of many voices, the upturning of many faces, the pressing on of many footsteps in the outskirts of the crowd, so that it swells forward in a mass, like one great heave of water, all flashes away. Twenty-Three.

They said of him, about the city that night, that it was the peacefullest man's face ever beheld there. Many added that he looked sublime and prophetic.

One of the most remarkable sufferers by the same axe—a woman—had asked at the foot of the same scaffold, not long before, to be allowed to write down the thoughts that were inspiring her. If he had given any utterance to his, and they were prophetic, they would have been these:

"I see Barsad, and Cly, Defarge, The Vengeance, the Jurymen, the Judge, long ranks of the new oppressors who have risen on the destruction of the old, perishing by this retributive instrument, before it shall cease out of its present use. I see a beautiful city and a brilliant people rising from this abyss, and in their struggles to be truly free, in their triumphs and defeats, through long, long years to come, I see the evil of this time and of the previous time of which this is the natural birth, gradually making expiation for itself and wearing out.

"I see the lives for which I lay down my life, peaceful, useful, prosperous and happy, in that England which I shall see no more. I see Her with a child upon her bosom, who bears my name. I see her father, aged and bent, but otherwise restored, and faithful to all men in his healing office, and at peace. I see the good old man, so long their friend, in ten years' time enriching them with all he has, and passing tranquilly to his reward.

"I see that I hold a sanctuary in their hearts, and in the hearts of their descendants, generations hence. I see her, an old woman, weeping for me on the anniversary of this day. I see her and her husband, their course done, lying side by side in their last earthly bed, and I know that each was not more honoured and held sacred in the other's soul, than I was in the souls of both.

"I see that child who lay upon her bosom and who bore my name, a man winning his way up in that path of life which once was mine. I see him winning it so well, that my name is made illustrious there by the light of his.

I see the blots I threw upon it, faded away. I see him, foremost of just judges and honoured men, bringing a boy of my name, with a forehead that I know and golden hair, to this place—then fair to look upon, with not a trace of this day's disfigurement—and I hear him tell the child my story, with a tender and a faltering voice.

"It is a far, far better thing that I do, than I have ever done; it is a far, far better rest that I go to, than I have ever known."

Questions

12. A Tale of Two Cities

1. Which of the following expressions best explains the meaning of the word *croaked* in the sentence: " 'It is a great pity,' croaked Jacques Three, dubiously shaking his head"?

   a. Jacques spoke in a low, hollow voice.
   b. His voice was hoarse.
   c. He spoke in a raucous, harsh tone foreboding evil like the cry of a raven.
   d. He grumbled.

2. What is the best explanation of the simile (in italics) in the following passage from selection 2: "The sawyer himself did not participate in the conference but abided at a little distance, *like an outer satellite* who was not to speak until required, or to offer an opinion until invited"?

   a. a moon revolving round a planet
   b. a servant to an important person
   c. a subservient follower
   d. an obsequious attendant awaiting his master's command

3. Which of the following traits of Sidney Carton's character is most forcefully brought out in selections 1 and 3 from *A Tale of Two Cities*?

    a. kindliness
    b. optimism
    c. sentimentality
    d. self-sacrifice

4. Which of the following definitions best describes the tone of the passages selected from Dickens' *Tale of Two Cities*?

    a. vengeful
    b. foreboding
    c. romantic
    d. hopeful

5. Which of the following words best summarizes Dickens' philosophy as revealed in the selections from *A Tale of Two Cities*?

    a. hope
    b. bitterness
    c. irony
    d. sympathy

6. Which of the following definitions best describes the development of *A Tale of Two Cities*?

    a. a romantic novel
    b. a serialized narrative
    c. a history of the 1790s
    d. a social criticism

13

W. Somerset Maugham

(1874-1965)

Of Human Bondage

Somerset Maugham, novelist and dramatist, was born in Paris where his father was a solicitor (lawyer) at the British Embassy. His family had practiced law in England for more than a hundred years.

His parents died when he was young, his mother of tuberculosis when he was eight, and his father of cancer two years later. He then went to live with a paternal uncle who was a vicar at Whitsable, a town near Canterbury.

From an early age Maugham had an irresistible inclination to write, but his uncle urged that he find a profession. He chose medicine and for five years studied at Saint Thomas's Hospital, London; in 1898 he qualified as a surgeon and physician but never practiced except as an intern in the slums of Lambeth. He still wanted to write!

For the next ten years, spent mostly in Paris, he wrote and almost starved, but good fortune finally came (and never left) with the performance of his first successful play, *Lady Frederick*. He wrote a succession of plays and was first known as a dramatist.

Now for a look backward: While still an intern at Saint Thomas's (1897-98), Maugham wrote an autobiographical novel and called it *The Artistic Temperament of Stephen Carey*. Unable to find a publisher who would pay £100 for it, Maugham fortunately kept the manuscript. Then, fourteen years later, after becoming a successful dramatist, he spent two years rewriting it. Upon completion, he entitled it *Beauty from Ashes*, a quotation from Isaiah; but upon discovering that another novel already bore the same title, he discarded it. This time he chose the name of one of the books in Spinoza's *Ethics*, and called it *Of Human Bondage*.

Of Human Bondage was first printed in England in early 1915, but did not gain popularity until it was published in the United States later that year. This, his greatest novel, is almost entirely autobiographical, except for the ending. Maugham said that he had to write this book to rid himself of the memories of an unhappy past that burdened him. When it was published, he said, "I found myself free forever from the pains and unhappy recollections that had tormented me."

By about six o'clock they were finished. Philip, exhausted by standing all the time, by the bad air, and by the attention he had given, strolled over with his fellow-clerks to the Medical School to have tea. He found the work of absorbing interest.... The directness of contact with men and women gave a thrill of power which he had never known. He found an endless excitement in looking at their faces and hearing them speak; they came in each with his peculiarity, some shuffling uncouthly, some with a little trip, others with heavy, slow tread, some shyly. Often you could guess their trades by the look of them. You learnt in what way to put your questions so that they should be understood, you discovered on what subjects nearly all lied, and by what inquiries you could extort the truth notwithstanding. You saw the different way people took the same things. The diagnosis of dangerous illness would be accepted by one with a laugh and a joke, by another with dumb despair. Philip found that he was less shy with these people than he had ever been with others; he felt not exactly sympathy, for sympathy suggests condescension; but he felt at home with them. He found that he was able to put them at their ease, and, when he had been given a case to find out what he could about it, it seemed to him that the patient delivered himself into his hands with a peculiar confidence.

"Perhaps," he thought to himself, with a smile, "perhaps I'm cut out to be a doctor. It would be rather a lark if I'd hit upon the one thing I'm fit for."

It seemed to Philip that he alone of the clerks saw the dramatic interest of those afternoons. To the others men and women were only cases, good if they were complicated, tiresome if obvious; they heard murmurs and were astonished at abnormal livers; an unexpected sound in the lungs gave them something to talk about. But to Philip there was much more. He found an interest in just looking at them, in the shape of their heads and their hands, in the look of their eyes and the length of their noses. You saw in that room human nature taken by surprise, and often the mask of custom was torn off rudely, showing you the soul all raw. Sometimes you saw an untaught stoicism which was profoundly moving. Once Philip saw a man, rough and illiterate, told his case was hopeless; and, self-controlled himself, he wondered at the splendid instinct which forced the fellow to keep a stiff upper-lip before strangers. But was it possible for him to be brave when he was by himself, face to face with his soul, or would he then surrender to despair? Sometimes there was tragedy. Once a young woman brought her sister to be examined, a girl of eighteen, with delicate features and large blue eyes, fair hair that sparkled with gold when a ray of autumn sunshine touched it for a moment, and a skin of amazing beauty. The students' eyes went to her with little smiles. They did not often see a pretty girl in these dingy rooms. The elder woman gave the family history, father and mother had died of phthisis, a brother and a sister, these two were the only ones left. The girl had been coughing lately and losing weight. She took off her blouse and the skin of her neck was like milk. Dr. Tyrell examined her quietly, with his usual rapid method; he told two or three of his clerks to apply their stethoscopes to a place he indicated with his finger; and then she was allowed to dress. The sister was standing a little apart and she spoke to him in a low voice, so that the girl should not hear. Her voice trembled with fear.

"She has not got it, doctor, has she?"

"I'm afraid there's no doubt about it."

"She was the last one. When she goes I shan't have anybody."

She began to cry, while the doctor looked at her gravely; he thought she too had the type; she would not make old bones either. The girl turned round and saw her sister's tears. She understood what they meant. The colour fled from her lovely face and tears fell down her cheeks. The two stood for a minute or two, crying silently, and then the older, forgetting the indifferent crowd that watched them, went up to her, took her in her arms, and rocked her gently to and fro as if she were a baby.

When they were gone a student asked:

"How long d'you think she'll last, sir?"

Dr. Tyrell shrugged his shoulders.

"Her brother and sister died within three months of the first symptoms. She'll do the same. If they were rich one might do something. You can't tell these people to go to St. Moritz. Nothing can be done for them."

Once a man who was strong and in all the power of his manhood came because a persistent aching troubled him and his club-doctor did not seem to do him any good; and the verdict for him too was death, not the inevitable death that horrified and yet was tolerable because science was helpless before it, but the death which was inevitable because the man was a little wheel in the great machine of a complex civilization, and had as little power of changing the circumstances as an automaton. Complete rest was his only chance. The physician did not ask impossibilities.

"You ought to get some very much lighter job."

"There ain't no light jobs in my business."

"Well, if you go on like this you'll kill yourself. You're very ill."

"D'you mean to say I'm going to die?"

"I shouldn't like to say that, but you're certainly unfit for hard work."

"If I don't work who's to keep my wife and the kids?"

Dr. Tyrell shrugged his shoulders. The dilemma had been presented to him a hundred times. Time was pressing and there were many patients to be seen.

"Well, I'll give you some medicine and you can come back in a week and tell me how you're getting on."

The man took his letter with the useless prescription written upon it and walked out. The doctor might say what he liked. He did not feel so bad that he could not go on working. He had a good job and he could not afford to throw it away.

"I give him a year," said Dr. Tyrell.

Questions

13. Of Human Bondage

1. Which facet of the word *bondage (Of Human Bondage)* is exemplified in this selection?
   a. bondage to human desires
   b. bondage to duty
   c. bondage to appetite
   d. bondage to economics

2. "The man was a little wheel in the great machine." The author used this expression to show that
   a. The rapid mechanization taking place in England was affecting the lives of people.
   b. This man was but a mere automaton, powerless to reason for himself.
   c. This man was "locked in" by circumstances that prevented his making a change, which could save his life.
   d. This man was an important cog in the big machine of business and civilization.

3. Which one of the following character traits of Philip is best brought out in this selected passage?
   a. perceptiveness
   b. shyness
   c. aloofness
   d. courageousness

4. Which of the following expressions best describes the tone of the episode of the two sisters, one of whom had phthisis (tuberculosis)?
   a. cold
   b. realistic
   c. pathetic
   d. fatalistic

5. Which of the following best tells of the philosophy in this selection?
   a. Man is born only to suffer.
   b. Man is basically a courageous creature.
   c. Life is made tolerable through medicine.
   d. Life is interesting and dramatic.

6. The author organizes and develops this selection by
   a. using examples, then drawing a conclusion
   b. stating ideas, then illustrating them by using examples
   c. putting forth logical arguments based on human nature
   d. describing a series of pathetic people to illustrate a moral

14

Margaret Mitchell

(1900-1949)

Gone With the Wind

Margaret Mitchell of Atlanta, Georgia, gained worldwide fame through the one novel she wrote, *Gone With the Wind*. She attended Washington Seminary, a private school for young ladies (1914-18), and Smith College, Northampton, Massachusetts, which she left after one year to care for her widowed father. From 1922 to 1926 she served as a feature writer on the staff of the *Atlanta Journal* before embarking on her ten-year program of researching and writing her remarkable fictionalized account of the Civil War and the Reconstruction Period, 1861 to 1872, from a southern viewpoint. *Gone With the Wind* is a monumental work of 1,037 pages (about 500,000 words) showing how people met the changing conditions during and following the destruction of Atlanta by Sherman's army. Miss Mitchell displays exceptional storytelling skill in the dramatic confrontations between her characters: Scarlett O'Hara, a mercenary Georgia belle; Rhett Butler, a swashbuckling blockade-runner; Melanie Wilkes, a conservative southern lady; and her husband, Ashley Wilkes, an idealistic intellectual. The development of Scarlett's character is partially indicated in the four selections for study that end, as does the book, with the question as to whether she and her third husband Rhett will ever meet again.

Published in June 1936, *Gone With the Wind* met with immediate and unprecedented success. One million copies were sold by December of that year (at $3 each); twelve million authorized copies in twenty-six languages were sold by 1965, plus untold millions of unauthorized editions, particularly in the Orient, thus setting an all-time record for a work of fiction. It received the 1937 Pulitzer Prize for Literature.

Reprinted from *Gone With the Wind* by Margaret Mitchell. Used by permission of Stephens Mitchell.

In December 1939 the motion picture of *Gone With the Wind* was premiered in Atlanta with elaborate ceremony. It won many awards and set new attendance records—25 million people saw it by June 1940, although it required four hours to view it, including a fifteen-minute break. In the picture Vivien Leigh as Scarlett O'Hara and Clark Gable as Rhett Butler helped immortalize Miss Mitchell's two leading characters. And the picture has had several revivals, all successful, and with the likelihood of repeated showings in the years ahead, just as sales of the book go on and on.

In the 1940s Miss Mitchell was unable to write another novel because she was swamped with correspondence and business arrangements concerning the book, foreign-publication contracts, the motion picture, public appearances, and Red Cross work during World War II. As a gracious southern lady she felt obliged to answer thousands of personal letters even though this meant her declining numerous offers to write magazine articles, short stories, and a possible sequel to *Gone With the Wind.* At the height of her popular esteem, her life was cut short by a tragic automobile accident in Atlanta, the city she loved.

I

Oh, some day! When there was security in her world again, then she would sit back and fold her hands and be a great lady as Ellen had been. She would be helpless and sheltered, as a lady should be, and then everyone would approve of her. Oh, how grand she would be when she had money again! Then she would permit herself to be kind and gentle, as Ellen had been, and thoughtful of other people and of the proprieties, too. She would not be driven by fears, day and night, and life would be a placid, unhurried affair. She would have time to play with her children and listen to their lessons. There would be long warm afternoons when ladies would call and amid the rustlings of taffeta petticoats and the rhythmic harsh cracklings of palmetto fans, she would serve tea and delicious sandwiches and cakes and leisurely gossip the hours away. And she would be so kind to those who were suffering misfortune, take baskets to the poor and soup and jelly to the sick and "air" those less fortunate in her fine carriage. She would be a lady in the true Southern manner, as her mother had been. And then, everyone would love her as they had loved Ellen and they would say how unselfish she was and call her "Lady Bountiful."

Her pleasure in these thoughts of the future was undimmed by any realization that she had no real desire to be unselfish or charitable or kind. All she wanted was the reputation for possessing these qualities. But the meshes of her brain were too wide, too coarse, to filter such small differences. It was enough that some day, when she had money, everyone would approve of her.

Some day! But not now. Not now, in spite of what anyone might say of her. Now, there was no time to be a great lady.

II

"They mean to stamp out the Ku Klux if it means burning the whole town again and hanging every male over ten. That would hurt you, Scarlett. You might lose money. And there's no telling where a prairie fire will stop, once it gets started. Confiscation of property, higher taxes, fines for suspected women—I've heard them all suggested. The Ku Klux—"

"Do you know any Ku Klux? Is Tommy Wellburn or Hugh or—"

He shrugged impatiently.

"How should I know? I'm a renegade, a turncoat, a Scallawag. Would I be likely to know? But I do know men who are suspected by the Yankee and one false move from them and they are as good as hanged. While I know you would have no regrets at getting your neighbors on the gallows, I do believe you'd regret losing your mills. I see by the stubborn look on your face that you do not believe me and my words are falling on stony ground. So all I can say is, keep that pistol of yours handy—and when I'm in town, I'll try to be on hand to drive you."

"Rhett, do you really—is it to protect me that you—"

"Yes, my dear, it is my much advertised chivalry that makes me protect you." The mocking light began to dance in his black eyes and all signs of earnestness fled from his face. "And why? Because of my deep love for you, Mrs. Kennedy. Yes, I have silently hungered and thirsted for you and worshiped you from afar; but being an honorable man, like Mr. Ashley Wilkes, I have concealed it from you. You are, alas, Frank's wife and honor has forbidden my telling this to you. But even as Mr. Wilkes' honor cracks occasionally, so mine is cracking now and I reveal my secret passion and my—"

"Oh, for God's sake, hush!" interrupted Scarlett, annoyed as usual when he made her look like a conceited fool, and not caring to have Ashley and his honor become the subject of further conversation. "What was the other thing you wanted to tell me?"

"What! You change the subject when I am baring a loving but lacerated heart? Well, the other thing is this." The mocking light died out of his eyes again and his face was dark and quiet.

"I want you to do something about this horse. He's stubborn and has got a mouth as tough as iron. Tires you to drive him, doesn't it? Well if he chose to bolt, you couldn't possibly stop him. And if you turned over in a ditch, it might kill your baby and you too. You ought to get the heaviest curb bit you can, or else let me swap him for a gentle horse with a more sensitive mouth."

She looked up into his blank, smooth face and suddenly her irritation fell away, even as her embarrassment had disappeared after the conversation about her pregnancy. He had been kind, a few moments before, to put her at her ease when she was wishing that she were dead. And he was being kinder now and very thoughtful about the horse. She felt a rush of gratitude to him and she wondered why he could not always be this way.

"The horse is hard to drive," she agreed meekly. "Sometimes my arms ache all night from tugging at him. You do what you think best about him, Rhett."

His eyes sparkled wickedly.

"That sounds very sweet and feminine, Mrs. Kennedy. Not in your usual masterful vein at all. Well, it only takes proper handling to make a clinging vine out of you."

She scowled and her temper came back.

"You will get out of this buggy this time, or I will hit you with the whip. I don't know why I put up with you—why I try to be nice to you. You have no manners. You have no morals. You are nothing but a— Well, get out. I mean it."

But when he had climbed down and untied his horse from the back of the buggy and stood in the twilight road, grinning tantalizingly at her, she could not smother her own grin as she drove off.

Yes, he was coarse, he was tricky, he was unsafe to have dealings with, and you never could tell when the dull weapon you put into his hands in an unguarded moment might turn into the keenest of blades. But, after all, he was as stimulating as—well, as a surreptitious glass of brandy!

During these months Scarlett had learned the use of brandy. When she came home in the late afternoons, damp from the rain, cramped and aching from long hours in the buggy, nothing sustained her except the thought of the bottle hidden in her top bureau drawer, locked against Mammy's prying eyes. Dr. Meade had not thought to warn her that a woman in her condition should not drink, for it never occurred to him that a decent woman would drink anything stronger than scuppernong wine. Except, of course, a glass of champagne at a wedding or a hot toddy when confined to bed with a hard cold. Of course, there were unfortunate women who drank, to the eternal disgrace of their families.

III

Rhett had stood, loving her, understanding her, ready to help. Rhett at the bazaar, reading her impatience in her eyes and leading her out in the reel, Rhett helping her out of the bondage of mourning, Rhett convoying her through the fire and explosions the night Atlanta fell, Rhett lending her the money that gave her her start, Rhett who comforted her when she woke in the nights crying with fright from her dreams—why, no man did such things without loving a woman to distraction!

The trees dripped dampness upon her but she did not feel it. The mist swirled about her and she paid it no heed. For when she thought of Rhett, with his swarthy face, flashing teeth and dark alert eyes, a trembling came over her.

"I love him," she thought and, as always, she accepted the truth with little wonder, as a child accepting a gift. "I don't know how long I've loved him but it's true. And if it hadn't been for Ashley, I'd have realized it long ago. I've never been able to see the world at all, because Ashley stood in the way."

She loved him, scamp, blackguard, without scruple or honor—at least, honor as Ashley saw it. "Damn Ashley's honor!" she thought. "Ashley's honor has always let me down. Yes, from the very beginning when he kept on coming to see me, even though he knew his family expected him to marry Melanie. Rhett has never let me down, even that dreadful night of Melly's reception when he ought to have wrung my neck. Even when he left me on the road the night Atlanta fell, he knew I'd be safe. He knew I'd get through somehow. Even when he acted like he was going to make me pay to get that money from him at the Yankee camp. He wouldn't have taken me. He was just testing me. He's loved me all along and I've been so mean to him. Time and again, I've hurt him and he was too proud to show it. And when Bonnie died— Oh, how could I?"

She stood up straight and looked at the house on the hill. She had thought, half an hour ago, that she had lost everything in the world, except money, everything that made life desirable, Ellen, Gerald, Bonnie, Mammy, Melanie and Ashley. She had to lose them all to realize that she loved Rhett—loved him because he was strong and unscrupulous, passionate and earthy, like herself.

"I'll tell him everything," she thought. "He'll understand. He's always understood. I'll tell him what a fool I've been and how much I love him and I'll make it all up to him."

IV

She had never understood either of the men she had loved and so she had lost them both. Now, she had a fumbling knowledge that, had she ever understood Ashley, she would never have loved him; had she ever understood Rhett, she would never have lost him. She wondered forlornly if she had ever really understood anyone in the world.

There was a merciful dullness in her mind now, a dullness that she knew from long experience would soon give way to sharp pain, even as severed tissues, shocked by the surgeon's knife, have a brief instant of insensibility before their agony begins.

"I won't think of it now," she thought grimly, summoning up her old charm. "I'll go crazy if I think about losing him now. I'll think of it tomorrow."

"But," cried her heart, casting aside the charm and beginning to ache, "I can't let him go! There must be some way!"

"I won't think of it now," she said again, aloud, trying to push her misery to the back of her mind, trying to find some bulwark against the rising tide of pain. "I'll—why, I'll go home to Tara tomorrow," and her spirits lifted faintly.

She had gone back to Tara once in fear and defeat and she had emerged from its sheltering walls strong and armed for victory. What she had done once, somehow—please God, she could do again! How, she did not know. She did not want to think of that now. All she wanted was a breathing space in which to hurt, a quiet place to lick her wounds, a haven in which to plan her campaign. She thought of Tara and it was as if a gentle cool hand were stealing over her heart. She could see the white house gleaming welcome to her through the reddening autumn leaves, feel the quiet hush of the country twilight coming down over her like a benediction, feel the dews falling on the acres of green bushes starred with fleecy white, see the raw color of the red earth and the dismal dark beauty of the pines on the rolling hills.

She felt vaguely comforted, strengthened by the picture, and some of her hurt and frantic regret was pushed from the top of her mind. She stood for a moment remembering small things, the avenue of dark cedars leading to Tara, the banks of cape jessamine bushes, vivid green against the white walls, the fluttering white curtains. And Mammy would be there. Suddenly she wanted Mammy desperately, as she had wanted her when she was a little girl, wanted the broad bosom on which to lay her head, the gnarled black hand on her hair. Mammy, the last link with the old days.

With the spirit of her people who would not know defeat, even when it stared them in the face, she raised her chin. She could get Rhett back. She knew she could. There had never been a man she couldn't get, once she set her mind upon him.

"I'll think of it all tomorrow, at Tara. I can stand it then. Tomorrow, I'll think of some way to get him back. After all, tomorrow is another day."

Questions

14. Gone With the Wind

1. Which of the following is the best definition of the word *surreptitious* as used by the author in the phrase: "as stimulating . . . as a surreptitious glass of brandy"?
   a. clandestine
   b. unauthorized
   c. secret
   d. obtained by stealth

2. Which of the following best expresses the author's meaning when she writes that Scarlett finds Rhett to be "as stimulating as—well, as a surreptitious glass of brandy"?
   a. She is thrilled by Rhett's attention, then angered by his sarcasm.
   b. She is pleased by Rhett's revealing his feelings, though mockingly.
   c. She feels the warmth of Rhett's protection.
   d. She is stimulated by meeting Rhett on the sly.

3. Which of the following character traits of Scarlett O'Hara is most clearly shown in the selection from *Gone With the Wind*?
   a. selfish and mercenary
   b. loving attention yet unappreciative
   c. self-reliant
   d. hot-tempered

4. Which of the following words best explains the tone of the passages selected from *Gone With the Wind*?
   a. sympathetic
   b. jovial
   c. sarcastic
   d. serious

5. Which of the following statements best illustrates the philosophy of these selections?
   a. A woman often underestimates her husband.
   b. A woman often takes her husband for granted.
   c. Tomorrow is another day.
   d. Failure of people to communicate leads to serious misunderstandings.

6. Which of the following expressions best describes the pattern of development of *Gone With the Wind*?
   a. a simple yarn of fairly simple people
   b. a romance
   c. a sensational novel
   d. a symbolic work

15

Emile Zola
(1840-1902)

The Attack
on the Mill

Emile Zola, a French novelist, was born in Paris, France. His mother was a native of France. His father, an engineer, was Italian.

When Emile was seven, his father died, leaving very little to his surviving wife and son. Emile and his mother left Paris, not to return until 1858. From 1860 to 1865, Emile Zola worked for Hachette Publishers. It was during this period that he began writing and selling verse and short stories to various publications and periodicals.

Around 1868, "he evolved a pseudo-scientific theory of the naturalistic novel."[1] At times, he documented his naturalistic works so extensively that this documentation worked to the detriment of his writings.

Noted for his powerful descriptions of vice and misery, Emile Zola turned his attention to writing about France during the Second Empire. Most of these works were written during the late 1880s and early 1890s.

During his last years—1894 to 1902—Zola left his focus on naturalism and centered his writing on timely problems of social and religious significance. In 1898 he became deeply interested in the famous Dreyfus trial and wrote an article defending the unfairly accused Dreyfus, "J'Accuse," which suddenly made him the subject of international attention. It was this dramatic attack on anti-Semitism in the French Army that won him his greatest and most lasting fame.

---

[1] Sir Paul Harvey and J. E. Heseltine, eds., *The Oxford Companion to French Literature* (New York: Oxford University Press, 1959), p. 763.

He continued his interest in social and religious problems until 1902, when he died at the age of sixty-two.

The historical setting for this selection is as follows: The attack on the mill, in the French village of Rocreuse, on the banks of the Moselle River in Lorraine, took place during the Franco-German War (1870–71), in which the French armies under Emperor Napoleon were decisively defeated.

In the first section quoted, a group of French soldiers are using the stone-walled mill, owned by Merlier, as a stronghold to withstand the German advance. In the mill are Francoise, Merlier's daughter, and her fiancé, Dominique, who has come from Belgium to live on a nearby piece of land willed to him by an uncle. Francoise and Dominique are to be married the next day.

I

There were two more deaths. The mattresses were torn to shreds and no longer availed to stop the windows. The last volley that was poured in seemed as if it would carry away the mill bodily, so fierce it was. The position was no longer tenable. Still, the officer kept repeating:

"Stand fast. Another half-hour yet."

He was counting the minutes, one by one. He had promised his commander that he would hold the enemy there until nightfall, and he would not budge a hair's breadth before the moment that he had fixed for his withdrawal. He maintained his pleasant air of good humor, smiling at Francoise by way of reassuring her. He had picked up the musket of one of the dead soldiers and was firing away with the rest.

There were four soldiers left in the room. The Prussians were showing themselves *en masse* on the other side of the Moselle, and it was evident that they might now pass the stream at any moment. A few moments more elapsed; the captain was as determined as ever, and would not give the order to retreat, when a sergeant came running into the room, saying:

"They are on the road; they are going to take us in the rear."

The Prussians must have discovered the bridge. The captain drew out his watch again.

"Five minutes more," he said. "They won't be here within five minutes."

Then exactly at six o'clock he at last withdrew his men through a little postern* that opened on a narrow lane, whence they threw themselves into the ditch, and in that way reached the forest of Sauval. The captain took leave of Father Merlier with much politeness, apologizing profusely for the trouble he had caused. He even added:

"Try to keep them occupied for a while. We shall return."

While this was occurring Dominique had remained alone in the hall. He was still firing away, hearing nothing, conscious of nothing; his sole thought

---

postern: back door

Reading for Ideas

was to defend Francoise. The soldiers were all gone, and he had not the remotest idea of the fact; he aimed and brought down his man at every shot. All at once there was a great tumult. The Prussians had entered the courtyard from the rear. He fired his last shot, and they fell upon him with his weapon still smoking in his hand.

It required four men to hold him; the rest of them swarmed about him, vociferating like madmen in their horrible dialect. Francois rushed forward to intercede with her prayers. They were on the point of killing him on the spot, but an officer came in and made them turn the prisoner over to him. After exchanging a few words in German with his men he turned to Dominique and said to him roughly, in very good French:

"You will be shot in two hours from now."

II

It was the standing regulation, laid down by the German staff, that every Frenchman not belonging to the regular army, taken with arms in his hands, should be shot. Even the *compagnies franches** were not recognized as belligerents. It was the intention of the Germans, in making such terrible examples of the peasants who attempted to defend their firesides, to prevent a rising *en masse*, which they greatly dreaded.

The officer, a tall, square man about fifty years old, subjected Dominique to a brief examination. Although he spoke French fluently, he was unmistakably Prussian in the stiffness of his manner.

"You are a native of this country."

"No, I am a Belgian."

"Why did you take up arms? These are matters with which you have no concern."

Dominique made no reply. At this moment the officer caught sight of Francoise where she stood listening, very pale; her slight wound had marked her white forehead with a streak of red. He looked from one to the other of the young people and appeared to understand the situation; he merely added:

"You do not deny having fired on my men?"

"I fired as long as I was able to do so," Dominique quietly replied.

The admission was scarcely necessary, for he was black with powder, wet with sweat, and the blood from the wound in his shoulder had trickled down and stained his clothing.

"Very well," the officer repeated. "You will be shot two hours hence."

Francoise uttered no cry. She clasped her hands and raised them above her head in a gesture of mute despair. Her action was not lost upon the officer. Two soldiers had led Dominique away to an adjacent room, where their orders were to guard him.

---

compagnies franches: independent companies.

III

"You had better think the matter over," the officer replied. "I shall have no trouble in finding some one else to render us the service which you refuse. I am generous with you; I offer you your life. It is simply a matter of guiding us across the forest to Montredon; there must be paths."

Dominique made no answer.

"Then you persist in your obstinacy?"

"Shoot me, and let's have done with it," he replied.

Francoise, in the distance, entreated her lover with clasped hands; she was forgetful of all considerations save one—she would have had him commit a treason. But Father Merlier seized her hands, that the Prussians might not see the wild gestures of a woman whose mind was disordered by her distress.

"He is right," he murmured, "it is best for him to die."

The firing party was in readiness. The officer still had hopes of bringing Dominique over, and was waiting to see him exhibit some signs of weakness. Deep silence prevailed. Heavy peals of thunder were heard in the distance, the fields and woods lay lifeless beneath the sweltering heat. And it was in the midst of his oppressive silence that suddenly the cry arose:

"The French; the French!"

It was a fact; they were coming. The line of red trousers could be seen advancing along the Sauval road, at the edge of the forest. In the mill the confusion was extreme; the Prussian soldiers ran to and fro, giving vent to guttural cries. Not a shot had been fired as yet.

"The French! the French!" cried Francoise, clapping her hands for joy. She was like a woman possessed. She had escaped from her father's embrace and was laughing boisterously, her arms raised high in the air. They had come at last, then, and had come in time, since Dominique was still there, alive!

A crash of musketry that rang in her ears like a thunderclap caused her to suddenly turn her head. The officer had muttered, "We will finish this business first," and, with his own hands pushing Dominique up against the wall of a shed, had given the command to the squad to fire. When Francoise turned, Dominique was lying on the ground, pierced by a dozen bullets.

She did not shed a tear; she stood there like one suddenly rendered senseless. Her eyes were fixed and staring, and she went and seated herself beneath the shed, a few steps from the lifeless body. She looked at it wistfully; now and then she would make a movement with her hands in an aimless, childish way. The Prussians had seized Father Merlier as a hostage.

It was a pretty fight. The officer, perceiving that he could not retreat without being cut to pieces, rapidly made the best disposition possible of his men; it was as well to sell their lives dearly. The Prussians were now the defenders of the mill, and the French were the attacking party. The musketry fire began with unparalleled fury; for half an hour there was no lull in the storm. Then a deep report was heard, and a ball carried away a main branch of the old elm. The French had artillery; a battery, in position just beyond the ditch where Dominique had concealed himself, commanded the main street of Rocreuse. The conflict could not last long after that.

Ah! the poor old mill! The cannon balls raked it from wall to wall. Half the roof was carried away; two of the walls fell in. But it was on the side toward the Moselle that the damage was most lamentable. The ivy, torn from the tottering walls, hung in tatters, debris of every description floated away upon the bosom of the stream, and through a great breach Francoise's chamber was visible, with its little bed, the snow-white curtains of which were carefully drawn. Two balls struck the old wheel in quick succession, and it gave one parting groan; the buckets were carried away down stream, the frame was crushed into a shapeless mass. It was the soul of the stout old mill parting from the body.

Then the French came forward to carry the place by storm. There was a mad hand-to-hand conflict with the bayonet. Under the dull sky the pretty valley became a huge slaughter pen; the broad meadows looked on in horror, with their great isolated trees and their rows of poplars, dotting them with shade, while to right and left the forest was like the walls of a tilting-ground enclosing the combatants, and in Nature's universal panic the gentle murmur of the springs and watercourses sounded like sobs and wails.

Francoise had not stirred from the shed where she remained hanging over Dominique's body. Father Merlier had met his death from a stray bullet. Then the French captain, the Prussians being exterminated and the mill on fire, entered the courtyard at the head of his men. It was the first success that he had gained since the breaking out of the war, so, all inflamed with enthusiasm, drawing himself up to the full height of his lofty stature, he laughed pleasantly, as a handsome cavalier like him might laugh. Then, perceiving poor idiotic Francoise where she crouched between the corpses of her father and her intended, among the smoking ruins of the mill, he saluted her gallantly with his sword, and shouted:

"Victory! Victory!"

Questions

15. The Attack on the Mill

1. Which of the following definitions best applies to the word *postern* in the phrase: "he at last withdrew his men through a little postern"?
   a. a window
   b. a back door
   c. a break in the wall
   d. a tunnel

2. When the author compares the wheel of the mill to its soul, which of the following best expresses his meaning?
   a. The mill almost seemed to be alive.
   b. The wheel was the life and essence of the mill.
   c. The mill became somewhat ghostlike.
   d. The wheel exemplified the death of nature and beauty.

3. Which of the following best describes the author's depiction of Dominique's character in the story?
   a. quiet courage
   b. daring heroism
   c. obstinate rebellion
   d. reckless fury

4. Which of the following expressions best describes the tone of the story?
   a. factual
   b. emotional
   c. critical
   d. impersonal

5. The author's philosophy in this story is that there is
   a. glory in courage
   b. no glory in war
   c. glory in victory
   d. no glory in heroism

6. Which of the following best describes the pattern of development?
   a. a moralistic tragedy
   b. a historical novel
   c. an exciting piece of fiction
   d. a factual account

16

Stephen Crane

(1871-1900)

The Red Badge
of Courage

Stephen Crane was born in Newark, New Jersey, the fourteenth child of
an old New Jersey family of Revolutionary descent. His father, a minister,
died in 1880; eleven years later, when Stephen, with one semester at
Syracuse University, was twenty years old, his mother died, leaving him to
shift for himself. As an aspiring young writer, he lived in The Bowery of New
York City where he nearly starved for three years until he became a
correspondent for the Bacheller Syndicate. This newspaper organization
published his *The Red Badge of Courage* in serialized form in 1894. This
novel, which appeared in book form in 1895, made Crane internationally
famous. Then followed *Maggie: A Girl of the Streets* and scores of short
stories but scant income.

Crane served as a correspondent in the Greco-Turkish War (1897) and
in the Spanish-American War in Cuba (1898). On August 25, 1898, he
married Cora Taylor, and, a few months later, moved to England where he
was recognized as a prominent literary figure. Here he lived happily, but he
overtaxed his strength writing to pay his debts and died of tuberculosis at
age twenty-eight in 1900.

In the selected passages taken from *The Red Badge of Courage* we do
not find the principal character to be a dashing, courageous hero of the
Romantics; rather we find an ordinary person—the youthful Henry—who
possesses the mixed and befuddled feelings of a real human being. In Henry

the author points out the fine line between bravery and fear. The author shows that the mind in panic releases a frenzied burst of energy that may drive the human machine either rearward or forward attacking any obstruction in its path.

The setting for these passages is a retreat during a battle in the Civil War.

I

Presently, men were running hither and thither in all ways. The artillery booming, forward, rearward, and on the flanks made jumble of ideas of direction. Landmarks had vanished into the gathered gloom. The youth began to imagine that he had got into the center of the tremendous quarrel, and he could perceive no way out of it. From the mouths of the fleeing men came a thousand wild questions, but no one made answers.

The youth, after rushing about and throwing interrogations at the heedless bands of retreating infantry, finally clutched a man by the arm. They swung around face to face.

"Why—why—" stammered the youth struggling with his balking tongue.

The man screamed: "Let go me! Let go me!" His face was livid and his eyes were rolling uncontrolled. He was heaving and panting. He still grasped his rifle, perhaps having forgotten to release his hold upon it. He tugged frantically, and the youth being compelled to lean forward was dragged several paces.

"Let go me! Let go me!"

"Why—why—" stuttered the youth.

"Well, then!" bawled the man in a lurid rage. He adroitly and fiercely swung his rifle. It crushed upon the youth's head. The man ran on.

The youth's fingers had turned to paste upon the other man's arm. The energy was smitten from his muscles. He saw the flaming wings of lightning flash before his vision. There was a deafening rumble of thunder within his head.

Suddenly his legs seemed to die. He sank writhing to the ground. He tried to arise. In his efforts against the numbing pain he was like a man wrestling with a creature of the air.

II

The youth's senses were so deadened that his friend's voice sounded from afar and he could scarcely feel the pressure of the corporal's arm. He submitted passively to the latter's directing strength. His head was in the old manner hanging forward upon his breast. His knees wobbled.

The corporal led him into the glare of the fire. "Now, Henry," he said, "let's have a look at yer ol' head."

The youth sat down obediently and the corporal, laying aside his rifle, began to fumble in the bushy hair of his comrade. He was obliged to turn the other's head so that the full flush of the fire light would beam upon it. He puckered his mouth with a critical air. He drew back his lips and whistled through his teeth when his fingers came in contact with the splashed blood and the rare wound.

"Ah, here we are!" he said. He awkwardly made further investigations. "Jest as I thought," he added, presently. "Yeh've been grazed by a ball. It's raised a queer lump jest as if some feller had lammed yeh on th' head with a club. It stopped a-bleedin' long time ago. Th' most about it is that in th' mornin' yeh'll feel that a number ten hat wouldn't fit yeh. An' your head'll be all het up an' dry as burnt pork. An' yeh may get a lot 'a other sicknesses, too, by mornin'. Yeh can't never tell. Still, I don't much think so. It's jest a damn' good belt on th' head, an' nothin' more. Now, you jest sit here an' don't move, while I go rout out th' relief. Then I'll send Wilson t' take keer 'a yeh."

The corporal went away. The youth remained on the ground like a parcel. He stared with a vacant look into the fire.

III

But the regiment was a machine run down. The two men babbled at a forceless thing. The soldiers who had heart to go slowly were continually shaken in their resolves by a knowledge that comrades were slipping with speed back to the lines. It was difficult to think of reputation when others were thinking of skins. Wounded men were left crying on this black journey.

The smoke fringes and flames blustered always. The youth, peering once through a sudden rift in a cloud, saw a brown mass of troops, interwoven and magnified until they appeared to be thousands. A fierce-hued flag flashed before his vision.

Immediately, as if the uplifting of the smoke had been prearranged, the discovered troops burst into a rasping yell, and a hundred flames jetted toward the retreating band. A rolling gray cloud again interposed as the regiment doggedly replied. The youth had to depend again upon his misused ears, which were trembling and buzzing from the *melee* of musketry and yells.

The way seemed eternal. In the clouded haze men became panicstricken with the thought that the regiment had lost its path, and was proceeding in a perilous direction. Once the men who headed the wild procession turned and came pushing back against their comrades, screaming that they were being fired upon from points which they had considered to be toward their own lines. At this cry a hysterical fear and dismay beset the troops. A soldier, who heretofore had been ambitious to make the regiment into a wise little band that would proceed calmly amid the huge-appearing difficulties, suddenly sank down and buried his face in his arms with an air of bowing to a doom. From another a shrill lamentation rang out filled with profane allusions to a general. Men ran hither and thither, seeking with their eyes roads of escape. With serene regularity, as if controlled by a schedule, bullets buffed into men.

The youth walked stolidly into the midst of the mob, and with his flag in his hands took a stand as if he expected an attempt to push him to the ground. He unconsciously assumed the attitude of the color bearer in the fight of the preceding day. He passed over his brow a hand that trembled. His breath did not come freely. He was choking during this small wait for the crisis.

His friend came to him. "Well, Henry, I guess this is good-by—John."

"Oh, shut up, you damned fool!" replied the youth, and he would not look at the other.

Questions

16. The Red Badge of Courage

1. Which of the following definitions best applies to the word *attitude* in the sentence: "He unconsciously assumed the attitude of the color bearer in the fight of the preceding day"?
   a. a state of mind
   b. a pose
   c. a posture
   d. a stand

2. When the author states: "But the regiment was a machine run down," which of the following best expresses his meaning?
   a. The men had run out of ammunition.
   b. The soldiers were tired and hungry.
   c. The morale of the unit had disintegrated.
   d. The caissons could no longer roll on.

3. Which of the following *best* depicts the character of Henry as he is shown in the selected passages?
   a. forlorn and helpless
   b. pathetic and weak
   c. fearless and bold
   d. questioning and bewildered

4. Which of the following best describes the tone of this passage from *The Red Badge of Courage*?
   a. philosophical
   b. emotive
   c. detached
   d. moralistic

5. Which of the following *best* describes the attitude expressed in this passage?
   a. In time of retreat it is every man for himself.
   b. Men all act identically under stress of war.
   c. War is senseless and cruel.
   d. War turns all men into animals.

6. Which of the following expressions best describes the pattern of development in this particular passage?
   a. a historical narrative of a battle retreat
   b. a chronological series of battle-retreat scenes
   c. a logically developed argument against war
   d. a study and comparison of bravery and cowardice

17

Ernest Hemingway

(1899-1961)

The Old Man and the Sea

Ernest Hemingway received the Pulitzer Prize in 1953 for *The Old Man and the Sea* which was published the preceding year. In 1954 he was awarded the Nobel Prize for Literature, an honor accorded to only five other American writers.

The Old Man and the Sea, of 26,531 words by the author's own count, is neither a short story nor a novel. It is a novella, and the last significant work of a man of action who, unlike most writers, has become a legend. He was a newspaper reporter, a soldier, and an ambulance driver wounded in World War I, an expatriate in Spain during the civil war, and a deep-sea fisherman in the Caribbean. With this background in mind, we can understand how he chose to write of common men in scenes of action (soldiers, bullfighters, hunters, and fishermen), and of how they conduct themselves under pressure. His informal, flat, terse prose is in the style of a trained newspaper correspondent; it is distinguished by limited use of adjectives and figures of speech, and by clipped, often single-word dialogue that reveals as much by what is unsaid as by what is spoken. Perhaps *The Old Man and the Sea* is somewhat lacking in the punch and freshness of Hemingway's earlier writing, but it is a powerful picture of a common man achieving uncommon bravery and dignity. To appreciate fully this achievement of Santiago's, as well as Hemingway's full statement of the gulf between man's hope and his fulfillment, the story should be read in its entirety.

Santiago, an old wornout Cuban fisherman, hooked onto the biggest marlin ever seen in the Gulf Stream off Cuba. After several days and nights of exhausting work, Santiago drew the fish alongside the boat, harpooned it, and lashed it to the side of his skiff. On his way to Havana harbor, the sharks closed in to tear the flesh, eventually leaving only the stripped skeleton of the marlin.

Arriving in the harbor, Santiago made his way to his shack and fell into a deep sleep. Meanwhile, local fishermen marveled at the skeleton of the record-sized marlin, eighteen feet long.

As we enter the story, we find that Santiago has already been battling the huge fish for almost twenty-four hours. Ordinarily, he is accompanied by his devoted protege, Manolin; but, after catching no fish for eighty or so days, the boy's parents had *ordered* him to go out to sea in luckier boats.

In the first section quoted, we find Santiago talking and thinking aloud. He is looking at the sky to judge the weather. In section 2, after having slept deeply, Santiago was cared for and fed by Manolin, and the two are already planning to fish again, this time together.

I

He looked at the sky and saw the white cumulus built like friendly piles of ice cream and high above were the thin feathers of the cirrus against the high September sky.

"Light *brisa*," he said. "Better weather for me than for you, fish."

His left hand was still cramped, but he was unknotting it slowly.

I hate a cramp, he thought. It is a treachery of one's own body. It is humiliating before others to have a diarrhea from ptomaine poisoning or to vomit from it. But a cramp, he thought of it as a *calambre*, humiliates oneself especially when one is alone.

If the boy were here he could rub it for me and loosen it down from the forearm, he thought. But it will loosen up.

Then, with his right hand he felt the difference in the pull of the line before he saw the slant change in the water. Then, as he leaned against the line and slapped his left hand hard and fast against his thigh he saw the line slanting slowly upward.

"He's coming up," he said. "Come on hand. Please come on."

The line rose slowly and steadily and then the surface of the ocean bulged ahead of the boat and the fish came out. He came out unendingly and water poured from his sides. He was bright in the sun and his head and back were dark purple and in the sun the stripes on his sides showed wide and a light lavender. His sword was as long as a baseball bat and tapered like a rapier and he rose his full length from the water and then re-entered it, smoothly, like a diver and the old man saw the great scythe-blade of his tail go under and the line commenced to race out.

"He is two feet longer than the skiff," the old man said. The line was going out fast but steadily and the fish was not panicked. The old man was trying with both hands to keep the line just inside of breaking strength. He knew that if he could not slow the fish with a steady pressure the fish could take out all the line and break it.

He is a great fish and I must convince him, he thought. I must never let him learn his strength nor what he could do if he made his run. If I were him I would put in everything now and go until something broke. But, thank God, they are not as intelligent as we who kill them; although they are more noble and more able.

The old man had seen many great fish. He had seen many that weighed more than a thousand pounds and he had caught two of that size in his life, but never alone. Now alone, and out of sight of land, he was fast to the biggest fish that he had ever seen and bigger than he had ever heard of, and his left hand was still as tight as the gripped claws of an eagle.

It will uncramp though, he thought. Surely it will uncramp to help my right hand. There are three things that are brothers: the fish and my two hands. It must uncramp. It is unworthy of it to be cramped. The fish had slowed again and was going at his usual pace.

I wonder why he jumped, the old man thought. He jumped almost as though to show me how big he was. I know now, anyway, he thought. I wish I could show him what sort of man I am. But then he would see the cramped hand. Let him think I am more man than I am and I will be so. I wish I was the fish, he thought, with everything he has against only my will and my intelligence.

He settled comfortably against the wood and took his suffering as it came and the fish swam steadily and the boat moved slowly through the dark water. There was a small sea rising with the wind coming up from the east and at noon the old man's left hand was uncramped.

"Bad news for you, fish," he said and shifted the line over the sacks that covered his shoulders.

He was comfortable but suffering, although he did not admit the suffering at all.

"I am not religious," he said. "But I will say ten Our Fathers and ten Hail Marys that I should catch this fish, and I promise to make a pilgrimage to the Virgin of Cobre if I catch him. That is a promise."

II

"Did they search for me?"

"Of course. With coast guard and with planes."

"The ocean is very big and a skiff is small and hard to see," the old man said. He noticed how pleasant it was to have someone to talk to instead of speaking only to himself and to the sea. "I missed you," he said. "What did you catch?"

"One the first day. One the second, and two the third."

"Very good."

"Now we fish together again."

"No. I am not lucky. I am not lucky anymore."

"The hell with luck," the boy said. "I'll bring the luck with me."

"What will your family say?"

"I do not care. I caught two yesterday. But we will fish together now for I still have much to learn."

"We must get a good killing lance and always have it on board. You can make the blade from a spring leaf from an old Ford. We can grind it in Guanabacoa. It should be sharp and not tempered so it will break. My knife broke."

"I'll get another knife and have the spring ground. How many days of heavy *brisa* have we?"

"Maybe three. Maybe more."

"I will have everything in order," the boy said. "You get your hands well, old man."

"I know how to care for them. In the night I spat something strange and felt something in my chest was broken."

"Get that well too," the boy said. "Lie down, old man, and I will bring you your clean shirt. And something to eat."

"Bring any of the papers of the time that I was gone," the old man said.

"You must get well fast for there is much that I can learn and you can teach me everything. How much did you suffer?"

"Plenty," the old man said.

"I'll bring the food and the papers," the boy said. "Rest well, old man. I will bring stuff from the drugstore for your hands."

"Don't forget to tell Pedrico the head is his."

"No. I will remember."

As the boy went out the door and down the worn coral rock road he was crying again.

That afternoon there was a party of tourists at the Terrace and looking down in the water among the empty beer cans and dead barracudas a woman saw a great long white spine with a huge tail at the end that lifted and swung with the tide while the east wind blew a heavy steady sea outside the entrance to the harbour.

"What's that?" she asked a waiter and pointed to the long backbone of the great fish that was now just garbage waiting to go out with the tide.

"Tiburon," the waiter said, "Eshark." He was meaning to explain what had happened.

"I didn't know sharks had such handsome, beautifully formed tails."

"I didn't either," her male companion said.

Up the road, in his shack, the old man was sleeping again. He was still sleeping on his face and the boy was sitting by him watching him. The old man was dreaming about the lions.

Questions

17. The Old Man and the Sea

1. When Hemingway titled his book *The Old Man and the Sea*, what was he saying about the old man's struggle?
    a. The old man fought a giant fish.
    b. The old man fought the fear and helplessness of isolation.
    c. The old man fought the weather and the sharks.
    d. The old man fought all of these things.

2. Which of the following best expresses the meaning of the metaphor: "There are three things that are brothers: the fish and my two hands"?
    a. The fish and his two hands are eager for each other.
    b. The fish and his two hands are all pulling together.
    c. The fish and his two hands are all bound together by line, pole, and hook.
    d. The fish and his two hands are all equally strong.

3. Which of these character traits of Santiago is most forcefully brought out in *The Old Man and the Sea*?
    a. religious
    b. courageous
    c. kindhearted
    d. generous

4. Which one of the following best describes the tone of *The Old Man and the Sea*?
   a. ironic
   b. satiric
   c. emotional
   d. sympathetic

5. Which of the following best tells of Hemingway's philosophy as revealed in the selections from *The Old Man and the Sea*?
   a. In order to defeat an adversary you must study him.
   b. A man who bears pain stoically is worthy of great respect.
   c. Bravery under stress is the highest accomplishment of a man.
   d. To capture a great fish, a man must be brutal and cruel.

6. Which of the following phrases best describes the pattern of development?
   a. a philosophical study
   b. an ironic tragedy
   c. a narrative
   d. a story of the sport of fishing

18

Herman Wouk

(1915-   )

The Caine Mutiny

A native of New York City, Herman Wouk graduated from Columbia University where he majored in comparative literature and philosophy. At Columbia he gained valuable experience in editing the college humor magazine and later became a scriptwriter for radio comedians, including the great Fred Allen.

From 1942 to 1946 Wouk served in the United States Navy, operating in the Pacific as executive officer of the destroyer-minesweeper *Southard*. Although the book is not autobiographical, he used his Navy background for *The Caine Mutiny* (published in 1951), which sold more than three million copies in English-language editions. Dramatized by Wouk for the Broadway hit (starring Henry Fonda), and made into a movie in 1954, the novel is considered by many as one of the best novels of World War II and was chosen by the Literary Guild. Its author was awarded the Pulitzer Prize in 1952.

In *The Caine Mutiny*, Wouk defied literary fashion for war novels by declaring his belief in (1) decency in language as well as deed, (2) honor, (3) duty, (4) responsibility, and (5) hallowed institutions like the United States Navy. After the sordid, world-weary, monosyllabic war novels that had appeared prior to *The Caine Mutiny*, Wouk's work brought in a freshness that was highly appreciated by the reading public.

The action portrayed in the following selection takes place in the South Pacific during World War II on board an old destroyer converted into a minesweeper, the *Caine*. The events in the story thus far indicate that the ship's captain, Lieutenant Commander Queeg, is a paranoid, a coward when facing the enemy, and tends to "freeze" when under extreme stress.

The action revolves around the following men: Lieutenant Steve Maryk, a professional fisherman in civilian life, is the executive officer (second in command); Lieutenant Willie Keith, a Princeton graduate, is on duty as OOD (officer of the deck); Stilwell, a gunner's mate second class, is the helmsman; Urban, a sailor, is the signalman; and "Sunshine" is the code name for the admiral's ship.

I

The storm's best recourse in the contest for the ship's life is old-fashioned bogeyman terror. It makes ghastly noises and horrible faces and shakes up the captain to distract him from doing the sensible thing in tight moments. If the wind can toss the ship sideways long enough it can probably damage the engines or kill them—and then it wins. Because above all the ship must be kept steaming under control. It suffers under one disadvantage as a drifting hulk, compared to the old wooden sailing ship: iron doesn't float. A destroyer deprived of its engines in a typhoon is almost certain to capsize, or else fill up and sink.

When things get really bad, the books say, the best idea is to turn the ship's head into the wind and sea and ride out the blow that way. But even on this the authorities are not all agreed. None of the authorities has experienced the worst of enough typhoons to make airtight generalizations. None of the authorities, moreover, is anxious to acquire the experience.

II

The *Caine* yawed shakily back and forth on heading 180 for a couple of minutes. Then suddenly it was flung almost on its beam-ends to port by a swell, a wave and a gust of wind hitting together. Willie reeled, brought up against Stilwell, and grabbed at the wheel spokes.

"Captain," Maryk said, "I still think we ought to ballast—at least the stern tanks, if we're going to steam before the wind."

Willie glanced at Queeg. The captain's face was screwed up as though he were looking at a bright light. He gave no sign of having heard. "I request permission to ballast stern tanks, sir," said the exec.

Queeg's lips moved. "Negative," he said calmly and faintly.

Stilwell twisted the wheel sharply, pulling the spokes out of Willie's hands. The OOD grasped an overhead beam.

"Falling off to *starboard* now. Heading 189—190—191—"

Maryk said, "Captain—hard left rudder?"

"Okay," murmured Queeg.

"Hard left rudder, sir," said Stilwell. "Heading 200—"

The exec stared at the captain for several seconds while the minesweeper careened heavily to port and began its nauseating sideslipping over the swells, the wind flipping it around now in the other direction. "Captain, we'll have to use engines again, she's not answering to the rudder. . . . Sir, how about heading up into the wind? She's going to keep broaching to with this stern wind—"

Queeg pushed the handles of the telegraph. "Fleet course is 180," he said.

"Sir, we have to maneuver for the safety of the ship—"

"Sunshine knows the weather conditions. We've received no orders to maneuver at discretion—" Queeg looked straight ahead, constantly clutching the telegraph amid the gyrations of the wheelhouse.

"Heading 225—falling away fast, sir—"

An unbelievably big gray wave loomed on the port side, high over the bridge. It came smashing down. Water spouted into the wheelhouse from the open wing, flooding to Willie's knees. The water felt surprisingly warm and sticky, like blood. "Sir, we're shipping water on the god-damn *bridge*!" said Maryk shrilly. "We've *got* to come around into the wind!"

"Heading 245, sir." Stilwell's voice was sobbing. "She ain't answering to the engines at all, sir!"

The *Caine* rolled almost completely over on its port side. Everybody in the wheelhouse except Stilwell went sliding across the steaming deck and piled up against the windows. The sea was under their noses, dashing up against the glass. "Mr. Maryk, the light on this gyro just went out!" screamed Stilwell, clinging desperately to the wheel. The wind howled and shrieked in Willie's ears. He lay on his face on the deck, tumbling around in the salt water, flailing for a grip at something solid.

"Oh Christ, Christ, Christ, Jesus Christ, save us!" squealed the voice of Urban.

"Reverse your rudder, Stilwell! Hard right! Hard right!" cried the exec harshly.

"Hard right, sir!"

Maryk crawled across the deck, threw himself on the engine room telegraph, wrested the handles from Queeg's spasmodic grip, and reversed the settings. "Excuse me, Captain—" A horrible coughing rumble came from the stacks. "What's your head?" barked Maryk.

"Two seven five, sir!"

"Hold her at hard right!"

"Aye aye, sir!"

The old minesweeper rolled up a little from the surface of the water.

Willie Keith did not have any idea of what the executive officer was doing, though the maneuver was simple enough. The wind was turning the ship from south to west. Queeg had been trying to fight back to south. Maryk was doing just the opposite, now; seizing on the momentum of the twist to the right and assisting it with all the force of engines and rudder, to try to swing the ship's head completely northward, into the wind and sea. In a calmer moment Willie would easily have understood the logic of the act,

The Caine Mutiny

but now he had lost his bearings. He sat on the deck hanging stupidly to a telephone jack-box, with water sloshing around his crotch, and looked to the exec as to a wizard, or an angel of God, to save him with magic passes. He had lost faith in the ship. He was overwhelmingly aware that he sat on a piece of iron in an angry dangerous sea. He could think of nothing but his yearning to be saved. Typhoon, *Caine*, Queeg, sea, Navy, duty, lieutenant's bars, all were forgotten. He was like a wet cat mewing on wreckage.

"Still coming around? What's your head? *Keep calling your head!*" yelled Maryk.

"Coming around hard, sir!" the helmsman screamed as though prodded with a knife. "Heading 310, heading 315, heading 320—"

"Ease your rudder to standard!"

"Ease the rudder, sir?"

"Yes, ease her, ease her!"

"Ru-rudder is eased, sir—"

"Very well."

Ease, ease ease—the word penetrated Willie's numb fogged mind. He pulled himself to his feet, and looked around. The *Caine* was riding upright. It rolled to one side, to the other, and back again. Outside the windows there was nothing but solid white spray. The sea was invisible. The forecastle was invisible. "You okay, Willie? I thought you were knocked cold." Maryk, braced on the captain's chair, gave him a brief side glance.

"I'm okay. Wha-what's happening, Steve?"

"Well, this is it. We ride it out for a half hour, we're okay— What's your head?" he called to Stilwell.

"Three two five, sir—coming around slower, now—"

"Well, sure, fighting the wind—she'll come around—we'll steady on 000—"

"Aye aye, sir—"

"We will not," said Queeg.

Willie had lost all awareness of the captain's presence. Maryk had filled his mind as father, leader, and savior. He looked now at the little pale man who stood with arms and legs entwined around the telegraph stand, and had the feeling that Queeg was a stranger. The captain, blinking and shaking his head as though he had just awakened, said, "Come left to 180."

"Sir, we can't ride stern to wind and save this ship," said the exec.

"Left to 180, helmsman."

"Hold it, Stilwell," said Maryk.

"Mr. Maryk, fleet course is 180." The captain's voice was faint, almost whispering. He was looking glassily ahead.

"Captain, we've lost contact with the formation—the radars are blacked out—"

"Well, then, we'll find them—I'm not disobeying orders on account of some bad weather—"

The helmsman said, "Steady on 000—"

Maryk said, "Sir, how do we know what the orders are now? The guide's antennas may be down—ours may be—call up Sunshine and tell him we're in trouble—"

Butting and plunging, the *Caine* was a riding ship again. Willie felt the normal vibrations of the engines, the rhythm of seaworthiness in the pitching, coming up from the deck into the bones of his feet. Outside the pilothouse there was only the whitish darkness of the spray and the dismal whine of the wind, going up and down in shivery glissandos.

"We're not in trouble," said Queeg. "Come left to 180."

"Steady as you go!" Maryk said at the same instant. The helmsman looked around from one officer to the other, his eyes popping in panic. "Do as I say!" shouted the executive officer. He turned on the OOD. "Willie, note the time." He strode to the captain's side and saluted. "Captain, I'm sorry, sir, you're a sick man. I am temporarily relieving you of this ship under Article 184 of *Navy Regulations.*"

"I don't know what you're talking about," said Queeg. "Left to 180, helmsman."

"Mr. Keith, *you're* the OOD here, what the hell should I do?" cried Stilwell.

Willie was looking at the clock. It was fifteen minutes to ten. He was dumfounded to think he had had the deck less than two hours. The import of what was taking place between Maryk and Queeg penetrated his mind slowly. He could not believe it was happening. It was as incredible as his own death.

"Never you mind about Mr. Keith," said Queeg to Stilwell, a slight crankiness entering his voice, fantastically incongruous under the circumstances. It was a tone he might have used to complain of a chewing-gum wrapper on the deck. "I told you to come left. That's an order. Now you come left, and fast—"

"Commander Queeg, you aren't issuing orders on this bridge any more," said Maryk. "I have relieved you, sir. You're on the sick list. I'm taking the responsibility. I know I'll be court-martialed."

Questions

18. The Caine Mutiny

1. In the second paragraph, the author says, "None of the authorities has experienced the worst of enough typhoons to make airtight generalizations." Which of the following definitions is most suitable for the word *airtight*?
   a. sealed
   b. glib
   c. pat
   d. infallible

2. The author says that in a contest for the ship's life, the storm uses "old-fashioned bogeyman terror." The author's purpose for using this figure of speech is
   a. to intensify, in the reader's mind, the terror of the scene being described
   b. to personify the storm, and make it seem that eerie, super-natural forces were at work
   c. to show Captain Queeg's terror of the storm
   d. to show that Maryk imagined the plight of the *Caine* to be worse than it really was

3. Maryk's action in taking command of the ship is proof of his
   a. disregard for authority
   b. overestimation of ability
   c. indifference to consequences
   d. concern for human life

4. Which of the following phrases best describes the tone of this selection?
   a. awesome
   b. suspenseful
   c. argumentative
   d. ironical

5. Which of the following best expresses the author's philosophical attitude?
   a. There is no justification for disobeying a senior officer.
   b. There are times when disobeying a senior officer is justifiable.
   c. A captain of a ship has no recourse but to follow orders.
   d. A captain of a ship may take action contrary to orders under certain circumstances.

6. The author develops this portion of his story by
   a. showing the battering power of the sea in a series of examples
   b. showing the intensity of the running argument between Captain Queeg and Maryk
   c. showing that the terror of the storm had overcome Captain Queeg
   d. showing a cause-effect relationship between the order given and the action of the ship

19

James Fenimore Cooper
(1789-1851)

The Last
of the Mohicans

James Fenimore Cooper, the first important American novelist, composed historical romances with settings principally in the heavily forested frontier of Northern New York. He lived as a country gentleman in Cooperstown on Lake Otsego, a village named for his father, and produced fifty literary works.

Best known are his Leatherstocking Tales: *The Pioneers* (1823), *The Last of the Mohicans* (1826), *The Prairie* (1827), *The Pathfinder* (1840), and *The Deerslayer* (1841). In this series of novels appear the heroic figures of a wilderness scout (called Hawkeye in *The Last of the Mohicans*) and his Indian friend Chingachgook (Delaware for Big Serpent). These two, with the latter's son, Uncas, are called upon to guide two English girls and their escort, Major Duncan Heyward, on a hazardous trip through the forest in *The Last of the Mohicans*. The time is 1757 during the French and Indian War. The girls, Cora Munro and her sister, Alice, seeking to join their father at Fort William Henry, depend for their very survival upon Hawkeye and his two Mohican aides. The story of their flight, their capture, and their escapes in a primitive country controlled by Montcalm and his savage Huron allies provides a thrilling historical romance and a revealing picture of the American Indian.

In section 1 of the passages chosen for study, Chingachgook sketches the history of the Indians. Sections 2 and 3 are two episodes in the flight and pursuit. Section 4 tells of an escape from one of the Hurons' attacks, while section 5 furnishes a fitting conclusion.

I

"A pine grew then where this chestnut now stands. The first palefaces who came among us spoke no English. They came in a large canoe, when my fathers had buried the tomahawk with the redmen around them. Then, Hawkeye," he continued, betraying his deep emotion only by permitting his voice to fall to these low, guttural tones, which rendered his language, as spoken at times, so very musical; "then, Hawkeye, we were one people, and we were happy. The salt lake gave us its fish, the wood its deer, and the air its birds. We took wives who bore us children; we worshipped the Great Spirit; and we kept the Maquas beyond the sound of our songs of triumph!"

"Know you anything of your own family at that time?" demanded the white. "But you are a just man, for an Indian! and, as I suppose you hold their gifts, your fathers must have been brave warriors, and wise men at the council fire."

"My tribe is the grandfather of nations, but I am an unmixed man. The blood of chiefs is in my veins, where it must stay forever. The Dutch landed, and gave my people the fire-water; they drank until the heavens and the earth seemed to meet, and they foolishly thought they had found the Great Spirit. Then they parted with their land. Foot by foot, they were driven back from the shores, until I, that am a chief and a sagamore, have never seen the sun shine but through the trees, and have never visited the graves of my fathers!"

"Graves bring solemn feelings over the mind," returned the scout, a good deal touched at the calm suffering of his companion; "and they often aid a man in his good intentions; though, for myself, I expect to leave my bones unburied, to bleach in the woods, or to be torn asunder by the wolves. But where are to be found those of your race who came to their kin in the Delaware country, so many summers since?"

"Where are the blossoms of those summers!—fallen, one by one: so all of my family departed, each in his turn, to the land of spirits. I am on the hill-top, and must go down into the valley; and when Uncas follows in my footsteps, there will no longer be any of the blood of the sagamores, for my boy is the last of the Mohicans."

"Uncas is here!" said another voice in the same soft, guttural tones, near his elbow; "who speaks to Uncas?"

The white man loosened his knife in his leathern sheath, and made an involuntary movement of the hand towards his rifle, at this sudden interruption; but the Indian sat composed, and without turning his head at the unexpected sounds.

At the next instant, a youthful warrior passed between them with a noiseless step, and seated himself on the bank of the rapid stream. No exclamation of surprise escaped the father, nor was any question asked, or

Reading for Ideas

reply given, for several minutes; each appearing to await the moment when he might speak, without betraying womanish curiosity or childish impatience. The white man seemed to take counsel from their customs, and, relinquishing his grasp of the rifle, he also remained silent and reserved. At length Chingachgook turned his eyes slowly towards his son, and demanded—

"Do the Maquas dare to leave the print of their moccasins in these woods?"

"I have been on their trail," replied the young Indian, "and know that they number as many as the fingers of my two hands; but they lie hid, like cowards."

"The thieves are out-lying for scalps and plunder!" said the white man, whom we shall call Hawkeye, after the manner of his companions. "That bushy Frenchman, Montcalm, will send his spies into our very camp, but he will know what road we travel!"

" 'Tis enough!" returned the father, glancing his eye towards the setting sun; "they shall be driven like deer from their bushes. Hawkeye, let us eat to-night, and show the Maquas that we are men to-morrow."

"I am as ready to do the one as the other; but to fight the Iroquois 'tis necessary to find the skulkers; and to eat, 'tis necessary to get the game—talk of the devil and he will come; there is a pair of the biggest antlers I have seen this season, moving the bushes below the hill! Now, Uncas," he continued in a half whisper, and laughing with a kind of inward sound, like one who has learnt to be watchful, "I will bet my charger three times full of powder, against a foot of wampum, that I take him atwixt the eyes, and nearer to the right than to the left."

"It cannot be!" said the young Indian, springing to his feet with youthful eagerness; "all but the tips of his horns are hid!"

"He's a boy!" said the white man, shaking his head while he spoke, and addressing his father. "Does he think when a hunter sees a part of the creatur', he can't tell where the rest of him should be!"

Adjusting his rifle, he was about to make an exhibition of that skill, on which he so much valued himself, when the warrior struck up the piece with his hand, saying—

"Hawkeye! will you fight the Maquas?"

"These Indians know the nature of the woods, as it might be by instinct!" returned the scout, dropping his rifle, and turning away like a man who was convinced of his error. "I must leave the buck to your arrow, Uncas, or we may kill a deer for them thieves, the Iroquois, to eat."

The instant the father seconded this intimation by an expressive gesture of the hand, Uncas threw himself on the ground, and approached the animal with wary movements. When within a few yards of the cover, he fitted an arrow to his bow with the utmost care, while the antlers moved, as if their owner snuffed an enemy in the tainted air. In another moment the twang of the cord was heard, a white streak was seen glancing into the bushes, and the wounded buck plunged from the cover, to the very feet of his hidden enemy. Avoiding the horns of the infuriated animal, Uncas darted to his side, and passed his knife across the throat, when bounding to the edge of the river it fell, dyeing the waters with its blood.

" 'Twas done with Indian skill," and the scout, laughing inwardly, but with vast satisfaction; "and 'twas a pretty sight to behold! Though an arrow is a near shot, and needs a knife to finish the work."

"Hugh!" ejaculated his companion, turning quickly, like a hound who scented game.

"By the Lord, there is a drove of them!" exclaimed the scout, whose eyes began to glisten with the ardor of his usual occupation; "if they come within range of a bullet I will drop one, though the whole Six Nations should be lurking within sound! What do you hear, Chingachgook? for to my ears the woods are dumb."

"There is but one deer, and he is dead," said the Indian, bending his body till his ear touched the earth, "I hear the sounds of feet!"

"Perhaps the wolves have driven the buck to shelter, and are following on his trail."

"No. The horses of white men are coming!" returned the other, raising himself with dignity, and resuming his seat on the log with his former composure. "Hawkeye, they are your brothers; speak to them."

II

Heyward, and his female companions, witnessed this mysterious movement with secret uneasiness; for, though the conduct of the white man had hitherto been above reproach, his rude equipments, blunt address, and strong antipathies, together with the character of his silent associates, were all causes for exciting distrust in minds that had been so recently alarmed by Indian treachery.

The stranger alone disregarded the passing incidents. He seated himself on a projection of the rocks, whence he gave no other signs of consciousness than by the struggles of his spirit, as manifested in frequent and heavy sighs. Smothered voices were next heard, as though men called to each other in the bowels of the earth, when a sudden light flashed upon those without, and laid bare the much-prized secret of the place.

At the farther extremity of a narrow, deep cavern in the rock, whose length appeared much extended by the perspective and the nature of the light by which it was seen, was seated the scout, holding a blazing knot of pine. The strong glare of the fire fell full upon his sturdy, weather-beaten countenance and forest attire, lending an air of romantic wildness to the aspect of an individual, who, seen by the sober light of day, would have exhibited the peculiarities of a man remarkable for the strangeness of his dress, the iron-clad inflexibility of his frame, and the singular compound of quick, vigilant sagacity, and of exquisite simplicity, that by turns usurped the possession of his muscular features. At a little distance in advance stood Uncas, his whole person thrown powerfully into view. The travellers anxiously regarded the upright, flexible figure of the young Mohican, graceful and unrestrained in the attitudes and movements of nature. Though his person was more than usually screened by a green and fringed hunting-shirt, like that of the white man, there was no concealment to his dark, glancing, fearless eye, alike terrible and calm; the bold outline of his high, haughty features, pure in their native red; or to the dignified elevation of his receding forehead, together with all the finest proportions of a noble head, bared to the generous scalping tuft. It was the first opportunity possessed by Duncan and his companions, to view the marked lineaments of either of their Indian attendants, and each individual of the party felt relieved from a burden of doubt, as the proud and determined, though wild expression of the features of the young warrior forced itself on their notice. They felt it might be a being partially benighted in the vale of ignorance, but it could not be one who would willingly devote his rich natural gifts to the purposes of wanton treachery. The ingenuous Alice gazed at his free air and proud carriage, as she would have looked upon some precious relic of the Grecian chisel, to which life had been imparted by the intervention of a miracle; while Heyward, though accustomed to see the perfection of form which abounds among the uncorrupted natives, openly expressed his admiration at such an unblemished specimen of the noblest proportions of man.

"I could sleep in peace," whispered Alice, in reply, "with such a fearless and generous looking youth for my sentinel. Surely, Duncan, those cruel murders, those terrific scenes of torture, of which we read and hear so much, are never acted in the presence of such as he!"

"This, certainly, is a rare and brilliant instance of those natural qualities, in which these particular people are said to excel," he answered. "I agree with you, Alice, in thinking that such a front and eye were formed rather to intimidate than to deceive; but let us not practice a deception upon ourselves, by expecting any other exhibition of what we esteem virtue than according to the fashion of a savage. As bright examples of great qualities are but too uncommon among Christians, so are they singular and solitary with the Indians; though, for the honor of our common nature, neither are incapable of producing them. Let us then hope that this Mohican may not disappoint our wishes, but prove, what his looks assert him to be, a brave and constant friend."

"Now Major Heyward speaks as Major Heyward should," said Cora; "who, that looks at this creature of nature, remembers the shade of his skin!"

A short, and apparently an embarrassed silence succeeded this remark, which was interrupted by the scout calling to them, aloud, to enter.

"This fire begins to show too bright a flame," he continued, as they complied, "and might light the Mingos to our undoing. Uncas, drop the blanket, and show the knaves its dark side. This is not such a supper as a major of the Royal Americans has a right to expect, but I've known stout detachments of the corps glad to eat their venison raw, and without a relish too. Here, you see, we have plenty of salt, and can make a quick broil. There's fresh sassafras boughs for the ladies to sit on, which may not be as proud as their my-hog-guinea chairs, but which sends up a sweeter flavor than the skin of any hog can do, be it of Guinea, or be it of any other land. Come, friend, don't be mournful for the colt; 'twas an innocent thing, and had not seen much hardship. Its death will save the creature many a sore back and weary foot!"

Uncas did as the other had directed, and when the voice of Hawkeye ceased, the roar of the cataract sounded like the rumbling of distant thunder.

"Are we quite safe in this cavern?" demanded Heyward. "Is there no danger of surprise? A single armed man, at its entrance, would hold us at his mercy."

A spectral-looking figure stalked from out the darkness behind the scout, and seizing a blazing brand, held it towards the farther extremity of their place of retreat. Alice uttered a faint shriek, and even Cora rose to her feet, as this appalling object moved into the light; but a single word from Heyward calmed them, with the assurance it was only their attendant, Chingachgook, who lifting another blanket, discovered that the cavern had two outlets. Then, holding the brand, he crossed a deep, narrow chasm in the rocks, which ran at right angles with the passage they were in, but which, unlike that, was open to the heavens, and entered another cave, answering to the description of the first, in every essential particular.

"Such old foxes as Chingachgook and myself are not often caught in a burrow with one hole," said Hawkeye, laughing.

III

He was interrupted by the low but expressive "Hugh!" of Uncas.

"I see them, boy, I see them!" continued Hawkeye; "they are gathering for the rush, or they would keep their dingy backs below the logs. Well, let them," he added, examining his flint; "the leading man certainly comes on to his death, though it should be Montcalm himself!"

At that moment the woods were filled with another burst of cries, and at the signal four savages sprang from the cover of the drift-wood. Heyward felt a burning desire to rush forward to meet them, so intense was the delirious anxiety of the moment; but he was restrained by the deliberate examples of the scout and Uncas. When their foes who leaped over the black rock that divided them, with long bounds, uttering the wildest yells, were within a few rods, the rifle of Hawkeye slowly rose among the shrubs, and poured out its fatal contents. The foremost Indian bounded like a stricken deer, and fell headlong among the clefts of the island.

"Now, Uncas!" cried the scout, drawing his long knife, while his quick eyes began to flash with ardor, "take the last of the screeching imps; of the other two we are sartain!"

He was obeyed; and but two enemies remained to be overcome. Heyward had given one of his pistols to Hawkeye, and together they rushed down a little declivity towards their foes; they discharged their weapons at the same instant, and equally without success.

"I know'd it! and I said it!" muttered the scout, whirling the despised little implement over the falls with bitter disdain. "Come on, ye bloody minded hell-hounds! yet meet a man without a cross!"

The words were barely uttered, when he encountered a savage of gigantic stature, and of the fiercest mien. At the same moment, Duncan found himself engaged with the other, in a similar contest of hand to hand. With ready skill, Hawkeye and his antagonist each grasped that uplifted arm of the other which held the dangerous knife. For near the minute they stood looking one another in the eye, and gradually exterting the power of their muscles for the mastery. At length, the toughened sinews of the white man prevailed over the less practised limbs of the native. The arm of the latter slowly gave way before the increasing force of the scout, who suddenly wresting his armed hand from the grasp of the foe, drove the sharp weapon through his naked bosom to the heart. In the meantime Heyward had been pressed in a more deadly struggle. His slight sword was snapped in the first encounter. As he was destitute of any other means of defence, his safety now depended entirely on bodily strength and resolution. Though deficient in neither of these qualities, he had met an enemy every way his equal. Happily, he soon succeeded in disarming his adversary, whose knife fell on the rock at their feet; and from this moment it became a fierce struggle, who should cast the other over the dizzy height into a neighboring cavern of the falls. Every successive struggle brought them nearer to the verge, where Duncan perceived the final and conquering effort must be made. Each of the combatants threw all his energies into that effort, and the result was, that both tottered on the brink of the precipice. Heyward felt the grasp of the other at his throat, and saw the grim smile the savage gave, under the revengeful hope that he hurried his enemy to a fate similar to his own, as he felt his body slowly yielding to a resistless power, and the young man experienced the passing agony of such a moment in all its horrors. At that instant of extreme danger, a dark hand and glancing knife appeared before him; the Indian released his hold, as the blood flowed freely from around the several tendons of the wrist; and while Duncan was drawn backward by the saving arm of Uncas, his charmed eyes were still riveted on the fierce and disappointed countenance of his foe, who fell sullenly and disappointed down the irrecoverable precipice.

"To cover! to cover!" cried Hawkeye, who just then had despatched the enemy; "to cover, for your lives! the work is but half ended!"

The young Mohican gave a shout of triumph, and, followed by Duncan, he glided up the acclivity they had descended to the combat, and sought the friendly shelter of the rocks and shrubs.

IV

"Extarminate the varlets! no quarter to an accursed Mingo!"

At the next moment, the breech of Hawkeye's rifle fell on the naked head of his adversary, whose muscles appeared to wither under the shock, as he sank from the arms of Duncan, flexible and motionless.

When Uncas had brained his first antagonist, he turned, like a hungry lion, to seek another. The fifth and only Huron disengaged at the first onset had paused a moment, and then seeing that all around him were employed in the deadly strife, he sought with hellish vengeance, to complete the baffled work of revenge. Raising a shout of triumph, he sprang towards the defence-less Cora, sending his keen axe, as the dreadful precursor of his approach. The tomahawk grazed her shoulder, and cutting the withes, which bound her to the tree, left the maiden at liberty to fly. She eluded the grasp of the savage, and reckless of her own safety, threw herself on the bosom of Alice, striving with convulsed and ill-directed fingers to tear asunder the twigs which confined the person of her sister. Any other than a monster would have relented at such an act of generous devotion to the best and purest affection; but the breast of the Huron was a stranger to sympathy. Seizing Cora by the rich tresses which fell in confusion about her form, he tore her from her frantic hold, and bowed her down with brutal violence to her knees. The savage drew the flowing curls through his hand, and raising them on high with an outstretched arm, he passed the knife around the exquisitely moulded head of his victim, with a taunting and exulting laugh. But he purchased this moment of fierce gratification with the loss of the fatal opportunity. It was just then the sight caught the eye of Uncas. Bounding from his footsteps he appeared for an instant darting through the air, and descending in a ball he fell on the chest of his enemy, driving him many yards from the spot, headlong and prostrate. The violence of the exertion cast the young Mohican at his side. They arose together, fought, and bled, each in his turn. But the conflict was soon decided; the tomahawk of Heyward and the rifle of Hawkeye descended on the skull of the Huron, at the same moment that the knife of Uncas reached his heart.

The battle was now entirely terminated, with the exception of the protracted struggle, between Le Renard Subtil and Le Gros Serpent. Well did these barbarous warriors prove that they deserved those significant names which had been bestowed for deeds in former wars. When they engaged, some little time was lost in eluding the quick and vigorous thrusts which had been aimed at their lives. Suddenly darting on each other, they closed, and came to the earth, twisted together like twining serpents, in pliant and subtle folds. At the moment when the victors found themselves unoccupied, the spot where these experienced and desperate combatants lay, could only be distinguished by a cloud of dust and leaves which moved from the centre of the little plain towards its boundary, as if raised by the passage of a whirlwind. Urged by the different motives of filial affection, friendship, and gratitude, Heyward and his companions rushed with one accord to the place, encircling the little canopy of dust which hung above the warriors. In vain did Uncas dart around the cloud, with a wish to strike his knife into the heart of his father's foe; the threatening rifle of Hawkeye was raised and suspended in vain, while Duncan endeavored to seize the limbs of the Huron with hands that appeared to have lost their power. Covered, as they were, with dust and blood, the swift evolutions of the combatants seemed to incorporate their bodies into one. The death-like looking figure of the Mohican, and the dark form of the Huron, gleamed before their eyes in such quick and confused succession, that the friends of the former knew not where nor when to plant the succoring blow. It is true there were short and fleeting moments, when the fiery eyes of Magua were seen glittering, like the fabled organs of the basilisk, through the dusty wreath by which he was enveloped, and he read by those short and deadly glances the fate of the combat in the presence of his enemies; ere, however, any hostile hand could descend on his devoted head, its place was filled by the scowling visage of Chingachgook. In this manner the scene of the combat was removed from the centre of the little plain to its verge. The Mohican now found an opportunity to make a powerful thrust with his knife; Magua suddenly relinquished his grasp, and fell backward without motion, and seemingly without life. His adversary leaped on his feet, making the arches of the forest ring with the sounds of triumph.

"Well done for the Delawares! victory to the Mohican!" cried Hawkeye, once more elevating the butt of the long and fatal rifle; "a finishing blow from a man without a cross will never tell against this honor, nor rob him of his right to the scalp."

But, at the very moment when the dangerous weapon was in the act of descending, the subtle Huron rolled swiftly from beneath the danger, over the edge of the precipice, and falling on his feet, was seen leaping, with a single bound, into the centre of a thicket of low bushes, which clung along its sides. The Delawares, who had believed their enemy dead, uttered their exclamation of surprise, and were following with speed and clamor, like hounds in open view of the deer, when a shrill and peculiar cry from the scout instantly changed their purpose, and recalled them to the summit of the hill.

" 'Twas like himself," cried the inveterate forester, whose prejudices contributed so largely to veil his natural sense of justice in all matters which concerned the Mingos; "a lying and deceitful varlet as he is. An honest Delaware now, being fairly vanquished, would have lain still, and been knocked on the head, but these knavish Maquas cling to life like so many cats-o'-the-mountain. Let him go—let him go; 'tis but one man, and he without rifle or bow, many a long mile from his French commerades; and, like a rattler that has lost his fangs, he can do no further mischief, until such time as he, and we too, may leave the prints of our moccasins over a long reach of sandy plain."

V

Chingachgook became once more the object of the common attention. He had not yet spoken, and something consolatory and instructive was expected from so renowned a chief on an occasion of such interest. Conscious of the wishes of the people, the stern and self-restrained warrior raised his face, which had latterly been buried in his robe, and looked about him with a steady eye. His firmly compressed and expressive lips then severed, and for the first time during the long ceremonies his voice was distinctly audible. "Why do my brothers mourn?" he said, regarding the dark race of dejected warriors by whom he was environed; "why do my daughters weep? that a young man has gone to the happy hunting-grounds; that a chief has filled his time with honor? He was good; he was dutiful; he was brave. Who can deny it? The Manitou had need of such a warrior, and He has called him away. As for me, the son and the father of Uncas, I am a blazed pine, in a clearing of the pale faces. My race has gone from the shores of the salt lake and the hills of the Delawares. But who can say that the serpent of his tribe has forgotten his wisdom? I am alone—"

"No, no," cried Hawkeye, who had been gazing with a yearning look at the rigid features of his friend, with something like his own self-command, but whose philosophy could endure no longer; "no, Sagamore, not alone. The gifts of our colors may be different, but God has so placed us as to journey in the same path. I have no kin, and I may also say, like you, no people. He was your son, and a red-skin by nature; and it may be that your blood was nearer—but, if ever I forget the lad who has so often fou't at my side in war, and slept at my side in peace, may He who made us all, whatever may be our color or our gifts, forget me! The boy has left us for a time; but, Sagamore, you are not alone."

Chingachgook grasped the hand that, in the warmth of feeling, the scout had stretched across the fresh earth, and in that attitude of friendship these two sturdy and intrepid woodsmen bowed their heads together, while scalding tears fell to their feet, watering the grave of Uncas like drops of falling rain.

In the midst of the awful stillness with which such a burst of feeling, coming, as it did, from the two most renowned warriors of that region, was received, Tamenund lifted his voice to disperse the multitude.

"It is enough," he said. "Go, children of the Lenape, the anger of the Manitou is not done. Why should Tamenund stay? The pale faces are masters of the earth, and the time of the red men has not yet come again. My day has been too long. In the morning I saw the sons of Unamis happy and strong; and yet, before the night has come, have I lived to see the last warrior of the wise race of the Mohicans."

Questions

19. The Last of the Mohicans

1. Which of the following is best described by the title of Cooper's novel *The Last of the Mohicans*?
   a. Uncas
   b. Chingachgook
   c. the end of the Mohican tribe
   d. the decline of the entire American Indian race

2. What is the best explanation of Cooper's use of the simile (in italics) when he writes, "There were short and fleeting moments when the fiery eyes of Magua were seen glittering, *like the fabled organs of the basilisk*"? (According to classical legend, the basilisk was a fabulous creature—dragon, lizard, and serpent—said to kill by its fiery look.)
   a. Magua tries to outstare Chingachgook.
   b. Magua tries to outstare his other enemies.
   c. Magua plans to "play dead."
   d. Magua merely shows his hatred.

3. Which of the character traits of the American Indian is most forcefully brought out in the selections from *The Last of the Mohicans*?
   a. boastfulness
   b. nobility
   c. resourcefulness
   d. ruthlessness

4. Which of the following definitions best describes the tone of the passages selected from *The Last of tne Mohicans*?
   a. venturesome
   b. romantic, in the sense of courtship
   c. foreboding
   d. confident

5. Which facet of the frontier scout Hawkeye's life is most clearly shown in the selections from *The Last of the Mohicans*?
   a. a hunter
   b. a woodsman
   c. a fighter
   d. a friend of the Mohicans

6. Which of the following phrases best describes the main theme of *The Last of the Mohicans*?
   a. the hazards of travel through the wilderness
   b. the cruel conduct of the Hurons
   c. the decline of the American Indian
   d. events of the French and Indian War

20

Leo Tolstoy

(1828-1910)

Anna Karenina

Leo Tolstoy, Russian author and moralist, was born into a noble family. He attended the universities of Kazan and Saint Petersburg, then in 1851 went into military service and had a distinguished record in the Crimean War. Thereafter for several years he traveled extensively throughout Western Europe and began his career of writing.

In 1861, the year of the liberation of the serfs, he returned to his estate, Yasnaya Polyana, in South Central Russia where he married Sofya Behrs and raised a family of thirteen children. Here, in comparative happiness, he managed his properties and resumed his writing. Here he produced his two great masterpieces *War and Peace* (1863-69) and *Anna Karenina* (1873-77). At this time and during the rest of his long life, he became more and more concerned with his inner life. So intense was his study of philosophy and theology, and so deep his probing into his own conscience, that at one time he contemplated suicide. He accepted the major tenets of Christianity but severely criticized the church and the state for protecting private property and for supporting the use of force.

His deep anxiety over spiritual problems tormented him and led him to give up his possessions, to dress like a peasant and work in the fields. He attracted many adherents to his belief in simple living, good deeds, and pacifism—even to his surprising disavowal of immortality, for which he was excommunicated from the church in 1901.

Finally at age eighty-two, estranged from his family who disapproved of his ascetic way of life, he wandered off, to be free of them, and died in a railroad station in remote Ryazan province.

Anna Karenina, from which six excerpts are here selected for study, is really a novel of two plots: one concerns the tragic relationships of Anna Karenina with her husband, Alexey Karenin, and her lover, Count Vronsky; the other plot tells the story of Konstantine Levin, a man whose happy married life and introspective nature parallel Tolstoy's own experiences in the first twenty years of his marriage.

I

When returning from the races Anna had informed him of her relations with Vronsky, and immediately afterwards had burst into tears, hiding her face in her hands. Alexey Alexandrovitch,* for all the fury aroused in him against her, was aware at the same time of a rush of that emotional disturbance always produced in him by tears. Conscious of it, and conscious that any expression of his feelings at that minute would be out of keeping with the position, he tried to suppress every manifestation of life in himself, and so neither stirred nor looked at her. This was what had caused that strange expression of deathlike rigidity in his face which had so impressed Anna.

When they reached the house he helped her to get out of the carriage, and making an effort to master himself, took leave of her with his usual urbanity, and uttered that phrase that bound him to nothing; he said that to-morrow he would let her know his decision.

His wife's words, confirming his worst suspicions, had sent a cruel pang to the heart of Alexey Alexandrovitch. That pang was intensified by the strange feeling of physical pity for her set up by her tears. But when he was all alone in the carriage Alexey Alexandrovitch, to his surprise and delight, felt complete relief both from this pity and from the doubts and agonies of jealousy.

He experienced the sensations of a man who has had a tooth out after suffering long from toothache. After a fearful agony and a sense of something huge, bigger than the head itself, being torn out of his jaw, the sufferer, hardly able to believe in his own good luck, feels all at once that what has so long poisoned his existence and enchained his attention, exists no longer, and that he can live and think again, and take interest in other things besides his tooth. This feeling Alexey Alexandrovitch was experiencing. The agony had been strange and terrible, but now it was over; he felt that he could live again and think of something other than his wife.

"No honor, no heart, no religion; a corrupt woman. I always knew it and always saw it, though I tried to deceive myself to spare her," he said to himself. And it actually seemed to him that he always had seen it: he recalled incidents of their past life, in which he had never seen anything wrong before—now these incidents proved clearly that she had always been a

---

*Alexey Alexandrovitch Karenin.

corrupt woman. "I made a mistake in linking my life to hers; but there was nothing wrong in my mistake, and so I cannot be unhappy. It's not I that am to blame," he told himself, "but she. But I have nothing to do with her. She does not exist for me. . . . "

Everything relating to her and her son, towards whom his sentiments were as much changed as towards her, ceased to interest him. The only thing that interested him now was the question of in what way he could best, with most propriety and comfort for himself, and thus with most justice, extricate himself from the mud with which she had spattered him in her fall, and then proceed along his path of active, honorable, and useful existence.

"I cannot be made unhappy by the fact that a contemptible woman has committed a crime. I have only to find the best way out of the difficult position in which she has placed me. And I shall find it," he said to himself, frowning more and more. "I'm not the first nor the last." And to say nothing of historical instances dating from the "Fair Helen" of Menelaus, recently revived in the memory of all, a whole list of contemporary examples of husbands with unfaithful wives in the highest society rose before Alexey Alexandrovitch's imagination. "Daryalov, Poltavsky, Prince Karibanov, Count Paskudin, Dram . . . Yes, even Dram, such an honest, capable fellow. . . . Semyonov, Tchagin, Sigonin," Alexey Alexandrovitch remembered. "Admitting that a certain quite irrational *ridicule* falls to the lot of these men, yet I never saw anything but a misfortune in it, and always felt sympathy for it," Alexey Alexandrovitch said to himself, though indeed this was not the fact, and he had never felt sympathy for misfortunes of that kind, but the more frequently he had heard of instances of unfaithful wives betraying their husbands, the more highly he had thought of himself. "It is a misfortune, which may befall any one. And this misfortune has befallen me. The only thing to be done is to make the best of the position."

II

The prince was anxious to miss nothing of which he would be asked at home, had he seen that in Russia? And on his own account he was anxious to enjoy to the utmost all Russian forms of amusement. Vronsky was obliged to be his guide in satisfying both these inclinations. The mornings they spent driving to look at places of interest; the evenings they passed enjoying the national entertainments. The prince rejoiced in health exceptional even among princes. By gymnastics and careful attention to his health he had brought himself to such a point that in spite of his excess in pleasure he looked as fresh as a big glossy green Dutch cucumber. The prince had traveled a great deal, and considered one of the chief advantages of modern facilities of communication was the accessibility of the pleasures of all nations.

He had been in Spain, and there had indulged in serenades and had made friends with a Spanish girl who played the mandolin. In Switzerland he had killed chamois. In England he had galloped in a red coat over hedges and killed two hundred pheasants for a bet. In Turkey he had got into a harem; in India he had hunted on an elephant, and now in Russia he wished to taste all the specially Russian forms of pleasure.

Vronsky, who was, as it were, chief master of the ceremonies to him, was at great pains to arrange all the Russian amusements, suggested by various persons to the prince. They had race-horses, and Russian pancakes and bear-hunts and three horse sledges, and gypsies and drinking feasts, with the Russian accompaniment of broken crockery. And the prince with surprising ease fell in with the Russian spirit, smashed trays full of crockery, sat with a gypsy girl on his knee, and seemed to be asking—what more, and does the whole Russian spirit consist in just this?

In reality, of all the Russian entertainments the prince liked best French actresses and ballet-dancers and white-seal champagne.

III

When Alexey Alexandrovitch with Lidia Ivanovna's help had been brought back anew to life and activity, he felt it was his duty to undertake the education of the son left on his hands. Alexey Alexandrovitch drew up a plan of education, and engaging the best tutor in Petersburg to superintend it, he set to work, and the subject continually absorbed him.

"You're coming to me," said Countess Lidia Ivanovna, "we have to speak of a subject painful to you. I have received a letter from her. She [Anna] is here in Petersburg."

"Who is to throw a stone?" said Alexey Alexandrovitch. "I have forgiven all, and so I cannot deprive her of what is exacted by her love for her son."

"I do not advise you to do this. If there were a trace of humanity left in her, she ought not to wish for it herself. No, I have no hesitation in saying I advise not, and if you will intrust it to me, I will write to her."

And Alexey Alexandrovitch Karenin consented, and Countess Lidia Ivanovna sent the following letter in French:

Dear Madame—To be reminded of you might have results for your son in leading to questions on his part which could not be answered without implanting in the child's soul a spirit of censure towards what should be for him sacred, and therefore I beg to interpret your husband's refusal in the spirit of Christian love. I pray to Almighty God to have mercy on you.

Countess Lidia

This letter attained the secret object which Countess Ivanovna had concealed from herself. It wounded Anna to the quick.

IV

"Dolly!"—she suddenly changed the subject—"you say I take too gloomy a view of things. You can't understand. It's too awful! I try not to take any view of it at all."

"But I think you ought to. You ought to do all you can."

"But what can I do? Nothing. You tell me to marry Alexey,* and say I don't think about it. I don't think about it!" she repeated, and a flush rose into her face. She got up, straightening her chest, and sighed heavily. With her light step she began pacing up and down the room, stopping now and then. "I don't think of it? Not a day, not an hour passes that I don't think of it, and blame myself for thinking of it . . . because thinking of that may drive me mad. Drive me mad!" she repeated. "When I think of it, I can't sleep without morphine. But never mind. Let us talk quietly. They tell me, divorce. In the first place, he won't give me a divorce. He's under the influence of Countess Lidia Ivanovna now."

Darya Alexandrovna, sitting erect on a chair, turned her head, following Anna with a face of sympathetic suffering.

"You ought to make the attempt," she said softly.

"Suppose I make the attempt. What does it mean?" she said, evidently giving utterance to a thought, a thousand times thought over and learned by heart. "It means that I, hating him, but still recognizing that I have wronged him—and I consider him magnanimous—that I humiliate myself to write him. . . . Well, suppose I make the effort; I do it. Either I receive a humiliating refusal or consent. . . . Well, I have received his consent, say . . . " Anna was at that moment at the furthest end of the room, and she stopped there, doing something to the curtain at the window. "I receive his consent, but my . . . my son? They won't give him up to me. He will grow up despising me, with his father, whom I've abandoned. Do you see, I love . . . equally, I think, both more than myself—two creatures, Seryozha and Alexey."

She came out into the middle of the room and stood facing Dolly, with her arms pressed tightly across her chest. In her white dressing-gown her figure seemed more than usually grand and broad. She bent her head, and with shining, wet eyes looked from under her brows at Dolly, a thin little pitiful figure in her patched dressing-jacket and night-cap, snaking all over with emotion.

"It is only those two creatures that I love, and one excludes the other. I can't have them together, and that's the only thing I want. And since I can't have that, I don't care about the rest. I don't care about anything, anything. And it will end one way or another, and so I can't, I don't like to talk of it.

---

*Alexey Vronsky.

So don't blame me, don't judge me for anything. You can't with your pure heart understand all that I'm suffering." She went up, sat down beside Dolly, and with a guilty look, peeped into her face and took her hand.

"What are you thinking? What are you thinking about me? Don't despise me. I don't deserve contempt. I'm simply unhappy. If any one is unhappy, I am," she articulated, and turning away, she burst into tears.

V

"I never boast, and I never tell lies," he said slowly, restraining his rising anger. "It's a great pity if you can't respect . . . "

"Respect was invented to cover the empty place where love should be. And if you don't love me any more, it would be better and more honest to say so."

"No, this is becoming unbearable!" cried Vronsky, getting up from his chair; and stopping short, facing her, he said, speaking deliberately: "What do you try my patience for?" looking as though he might have said much more, but was restraining himself. "It has limits."

"What do you mean by that?" she cried, looking with terror at the undisguised hatred in his whole face, and especially in his cruel, menacing eyes.

"I mean to say . . . " he was beginning, but he checked himself. "I must ask what it is you want of me?"

"What can I want? All I can want is that you should not desert me, as you think of doing," she said, understanding all he had not uttered. "But that I don't want; that's secondary. I want love, and there is none. So then all is over."

She turned towards the door.

"Stop! sto—op!" said Vronsky, with no change in the gloomy lines of his brows, though he held her by the hand. "What is it all about? I said that we must put off going for three days, and on that you told me I was lying, that I was not an honourable man."

"Yes, and I repeat that the man who reproaches me with having sacrificed everything for me," she said, recalling the words of a still earlier quarrel, "that he's worse than a dishonourable man—he's a heartless man."

"Oh, there are limits to endurance!" he cried, and hastily let go her hand.

"He hates me, that's clear," she thought, and in silence, without looking round, she walked with faltering steps out of the room. "He loves another woman, that's even clearer," she said to herself as she went into her own room. "I want love, and there is none. So, then, all is over." She repeated the words she had said, "and it must be ended."

"But how?" she asked herself, and she sat down in a low chair before the looking-glass.

Reading for Ideas

Thoughts of where she would go now, whether to the aunt who had brought her up, to Dolly, or simply alone abroad, and of what *he* was doing now alone in his study; whether this was the final quarrel, or whether reconciliation were still possible; and of what all her old friends at Petersburg would say of her now; and of how Alexey Alexandrovitch would look at it, and many other ideas of what would happen now after this rupture, came into her head; but she did not give herself up to them with all her heart. At the bottom of her heart was some obscure idea that alone interested her, but she could not get a clear sight of it. Thinking once more of Alexey Alexandrovitch, she recalled the time of her illness after her confinement, and the feeling which never left her at that time. "Why didn't I die?" and the words and the feeling of that time came back to her. And all at once she knew what was in her soul. Yes, it was that idea which alone solved all. "Yes, to die! . . . And the shame and disgrace of Alexey Alexandrovitch and of Seryozha, and my awful shame, it will all be saved by death. To die! and he will feel remorse; will be sorry; will love me; he will suffer on my account." With the trace of a smile of commiseration for herself she sat down in the armchair, taking off and putting on the rings on her left hand, vividly picturing from different sides his feelings after her death.

VI

These doubts fretted and harassed him, growing weaker or stronger from time to time, but never leaving him.* He read and thought, and the more he read and the more he thought, the further he felt from the aim he was pursuing.

Of late in Moscow and in the country, since he had become convinced that he would find no solution in the materialists, he had read and reread thoroughly Plato, Spinoza, Kant, Schelling, Hegel, and Schopenhauer, the philosophers who gave a non-materialistic explanation of life.

Their ideas seemed to him fruitful when he was reading or was himself seeking arguments to refute other theories, especially those of the materialists; but as soon as he began to read or sought for himself a solution of problems, the same thing always happened. As long as he followed the fixed definition of obscure words such as *spirit, will, freedom, essence,* purposely letting himself go into the snare of words the philosophers set for him he seemed to comprehend something. But he had only to forget the artificial train of reasoning, and to turn from life itself to what had satisfied him while thinking in accordance with the fixed definitions, and all this artificial edifice fell to pieces at once like a house of cards, and it became clear that the edifice had been built up out of those transposed words, apart from anything in life more important than reason.

---

*Konstantine Levin.

At one time, reading Schopenhauer, he put in place of his *will* the word *love*, and for a couple of days this new philosophy charmed him, till he removed a little away from it. But then, when he turned from life itself to glance at it again, it fell away too, and proved to be the same muslin garment with no warmth in it.

His brother Sergey Ivanovitch advised him to read the theological works of Homiakov. Levin read the second volume of Homiakov's works, and in spite of the elegant epigrammatic, argumentative style which at first repelled him, he was impressed by the doctrine of the church he found in them. He was struck at first by the idea that the apprehension of divine truths had not been vouchsafed to man, but to a corporation of men bound together by love—to the church. What delighted him was the thought how much easier it was to believe in a still existing living church, embracing all the beliefs of men, and having God at its head, and therefore holy and infallible, and from it to accept the faith in God, in the creation, the fall, the redemption, than to begin with God, a mysterious, far-away God, the creation, etc. But afterwards, on reading a Catholic writer's history of the church, and then a Greek orthodox writer's history of the church, and seeing that the two churches, in their very conception infallible, each deny the authority of the other, Homiakov's doctrine of the church lost all its charm for him, and this edifice crumbled into dust like the philosophers' edifices.

All that spring he was not himself, and went through fearful moments of horror.

"Without knowing what I am and why I am here, life's impossible; and that I can't know, and so I can't live," Levin said to himself.

"In infinite time, in infinite matter, in infinite space, is formed a bubble-organism, and that bubble lasts a while and bursts, and that bubble is Me."

It was an agonizing error, but it was the sole logical result of ages of human thought in that direction.

This was the ultimate belief on which all the systems elaborated by human thought in almost all their ramifications rested. It was the prevalent conviction, and of all other explanations Levin had unconsciously, not knowing when or how, chosen it, as any way the clearest, and made it his own.

But it was not merely a falsehood, it was the cruel jeer of some wicked power, some evil, hateful power, to whom one could not submit.

He must escape from this power. And the means of escape every man had in his own hands. He had but to cut short this dependence on evil. And there was one means—death.

And Levin, a happy father and husband, in perfect health, was several times so near suicide that he hid the cord that he might not be tempted to hang himself, and was afraid to go out with his gun for fear of shooting himself.

But Levin did not shoot himself, and did not hang himself; he went on living.

Questions

20. Anna Karenina

1. Which of the following definitions most aptly describes what Tolstoy had in mind in using the word *bubble* when he wrote Levin's thought on life: " 'In infinite time, in infinite matter, in infinite space, is formed a bubble-organism, and that bubble lasts a while and bursts, and that bubble is Me' "?

   a. Man is like an effervescence.
   b. Man is a delusion.
   c. Man lacks substance or firmness.
   d. Man lacks permanence.

2. Which of the following statements best explains Karenin's allusion to the "Fair Helen" of Menelaus in section 1?

   a. Karenin referred to Helen of Troy's unfaithfulness.
   b. He referred to her abduction.
   c. He wanted to refer to a case of a man bereft of his wife and followed by a reconciliation.
   d. He knew that Menelaus lost his wife but he (Karenin) was not sure of the circumstances.

3. Which of Anna Karenina's traits of character is most clearly shown in the selected passages?

   a. emotionalism
   b. quarrelsomeness
   c. jealousy
   d. despondency

4. Which of the following definitions of the author's tone is most forcefully stressed in the selection from *Anna Karenina*?
   a. logical
   b. figurative
   c. moralistic
   d. emotive

5. Which of the following statements best illustrates Leo Tolstoy's philosophy in the selection?
   a. A society can be dominated by the principle of self-pleasure.
   b. A married woman who becomes unfaithful fails to foresee the consequences.
   c. Hypocrisy is detestable and sinful.
   d. Man is engaged in a futile search for the meaning of life.

6. Which of the following definitions best describes the pattern of development of Tolstoy's *Anna Karenina*?
   a. character development through dialogue
   b. a portrayal of the characters' innermost thoughts
   c. social criticism
   d. a realistic novel of manners

AN ADDITIONAL WAY TO USE THIS BOOK

The Diagnostic Chart

Fast and sure improvement in reading comprehension can be made by using the Diagnostic Chart to identify your relative strengths and weaknesses. The Diagnostic Chart is, perhaps, the most direct and efficient instrument of its kind yet devised. Here is why and how it works.

The questions for every selection are always in the same order. For example, the question designed to teach the skill of "Recognizing Traits of Character" is always in the number three position, and the question designed to teach "Recognizing Tone" is always in the number four position, and so on. This innovation of ordering the questions sets the stage for the functioning of the Diagnostic Chart.

All you need to do is to place the letters of your answers in the proper blocks on the Diagnostic Chart. Even after completing one selection, the chart will reveal the types of questions you answered correctly, as well as the types answered incorrectly. But more important, it will identify the types of questions that you consistently miss. Such identification is possible after you have completed three or more selections. By then, you will be able to observe a pattern. For example, if the answers to question number four (Recognizing Tone) were incorrect for all three selections, or on three out of four, your weakness would be obvious.

Once a weakness in ascertaining tone is uncovered, you are urged to take the following steps: First, turn back to the instructional pages to study the section in which the topic of tone is discussed. Second, go back to reread, one at a time, the questions that you missed; then, with the correct answer in mind, reread the entire selection trying to perceive how the author developed the tone for the selection. Third, on succeeding selections, put forth extra effort to answer correctly the questions pertaining to tone. Fourth, if the difficulty still persists, arrange for a conference with your instructor.

DIAGNOSTIC CHART*

Categories of Comprehension Skills	Reading Passages																			
	1	2	3	4	5	6	7	8	9	10	11	12	13	14	15	16	17	18	19	20
1. Understanding the Author's Use of Words																				
2. Understanding the Author's Use of Figurative Language																				
3. Recognizing Traits of Character																				
4. Recognizing Tone																				
5. Recognizing the Author's Theme or Themes																				
6. Recognizing Development of the Theme																				
Comprehension Score (%)																				

*Record answers vertically.

Scoring Chart	
Number Right	Comprehension Score
1	17%
2	33%
3	50%
4	67%
5	83%
6	100%

Just as this book is designed to improve your comprehension skills in reading imaginative prose, a companion book, *Reading for Facts* (New York: David McKay Co., 1974), has been designed to improve your comprehension skills in reading factual prose.